EMOTIONAL INTELLIGENCE UNLOCKED

TRANSFORM YOUR RELATIONSHIPS, INCREASE YOUR SUCCESS AT WORK AND CONQUER YOUR SOCIAL SKILLS WITH PROVEN EQ STRATEGIES THAT ANYONE CAN USE TO GET THE LIFE THEY WANT

LIAM GRANT D.

© **Copyright 2024 - Liam Grant - All rights reserved.**

The content within this book may not be reproduced, duplicated or transmitted without direct written permission from the author or the publisher.

Under no circumstances will any blame or legal responsibility be held against the publisher, or author, for any damages, reparation, or monetary loss due to the information contained within this book. Either directly or indirectly. You are responsible for your own choices, actions, and results.

Legal Notice:

This book is copyright protected. This book is only for personal use. You cannot amend, distribute, sell, use, quote or paraphrase any part, of the content within this book, without the consent of the author or publisher.

Disclaimer Notice:

Please note the information contained within this document is for educational and entertainment purposes only. All effort has been expended to present accurate, up-to-date, and reliable, complete information. No warranties of any kind are declared or implied. Readers acknowledge that the author is not engaging in the rendering of legal, financial, medical or professional advice. The content within this book has been derived from various sources. Please consult a licensed professional before attempting any techniques outlined in this book.

By reading this document, the reader agrees that under no circumstances is the author responsible for any losses, direct or indirect, which are incurred as a result of the use of the information contained within this document, including, but not limited to, — errors, omissions, or inaccuracies.

TABLE OF CONTENTS

Introduction	7
1. FOUNDATIONS OF EMOTIONAL INTELLIGENCE	9
The Science Behind Emotional Intelligence: Debunking Myths	9
Measuring Your Emotional Quotient: The First Step to Growth	11
The Five Components of EQ Explained	16
Emotional Intelligence versus IQ: Why EQ Matters More in Relationships	20
2. SELF-AWARENESS MASTERY	25
Identifying Your Emotional Triggers	25
The Power of Journaling for Emotional Insight	27
Using Mindfulness to Enhance Self-Awareness	30
Feedback Loops: How to Use Them to Your Advantage	32
3. MANAGING YOUR EMOTIONS	35
Strategies for Cooling Down When You're Overwhelmed	35
The Role of Physical Exercise in Emotional Regulation	38
Creating Your Emotional Emergency Kit	40
Navigating Emotional Highs and Lows with Grace	43
4. MOTIVATION AND EMOTIONAL INTELLIGENCE	47
Setting EQ-Driven Goals	47
The Relationship Between Motivation and Emotional State	50
Overcoming Procrastination Through Emotional Awareness	52
EQ Techniques for Sustaining Motivation	55
5. EMPATHY—THE HEART OF CONNECTION	59
Active Listening Skills for Empathetic Engagement	60
Reading and Responding to Nonverbal Cues	62

Empathy in Conflict Resolution	65
Building Empathy in Digital Communications	67
6. COMMUNICATION MASTERY WITH EQ	73
The Art of Emotional Articulation	73
Assertive Communication: Speaking Your Truth without Harm	76
The Power of Vulnerability in Deepening Connections	78
Transformative Conversations: EQ Techniques That Facilitate Change	81
7. BUILDING AND MAINTAINING PERSONAL RELATIONSHIPS	85
EQ Strategies for Romantic Partnerships	85
Navigating Family Dynamics with Emotional Intelligence	88
Deepening Friendships with Emotional Awareness	90
Handling Breakups and Loss through EQ	92
8. EMOTIONAL INTELLIGENCE IN THE WORKPLACE	97
Leading with Emotional Intelligence: A New Paradigm	98
EQ in Team Dynamics: Fostering Harmony and Productivity	100
Managing Upward: EQ Strategies for Dealing with Supervisors	102
Navigating Office Politics with Grace and Wisdom	104
9. DEALING WITH DIFFICULT EMOTIONS	107
The EQ Approach to Managing Anger	107
Overcoming Anxiety with Emotional Intelligence	109
The Role of EQ in Treating Depression	111
Turning Envy and Jealousy into Growth Opportunities	114
10. EMOTIONAL INTELLIGENCE AND SOCIAL MEDIA	117
Protecting Your Emotional Health Online	117
Empathy and Kindness in Digital Interactions	120
Setting Boundaries: The EQ Way to Manage Social Media	122

From Online to In-Person: Translating EQ across
Platforms ... 124

11. BUILDING RESILIENCE THROUGH EMOTIONAL
INTELLIGENCE ... 129
The EQ Blueprint for Resilience ... 129
Learning from Failure: An EQ Perspective ... 132
The Role of Support Systems in Emotional
Resilience ... 134
Cultivating Hope and Optimism with EQ ... 136

12. A LIFELONG JOURNEY OF EMOTIONAL
INTELLIGENCE ... 141
Setting Up Your EQ Development Plan ... 141
Mindfulness Practices for Continuous EQ Growth ... 143
The Role of Mentorship in EQ Development ... 146
Celebrating Your Emotional Intelligence Milestones ... 148

Conclusion ... 153
Bibliography ... 157

INTRODUCTION

Have you ever wondered why some people navigate the complexities of relationships and professional challenges with remarkable ease? The secret often lies in what they know, how they relate to others, and how they understand themselves. This key, often overlooked, is emotional intelligence (EQ).

Research consistently shows high EQ scores are linked to more successful careers, deeper personal relationships, and enhanced overall well-being. For instance, studies indicate that people with higher emotional intelligence tend to have better work performance and more satisfying interpersonal relationships. This isn't just about having an edge at work or making friends easily—it's about cultivating a life filled with more understanding, empathy, and connectivity.

Let me share a personal story. I recall a time when my struggle to manage my emotions almost led to the loss of a cherished friendship. It was a moment of intense disagreement, and instead of addressing my feelings constructively, I allowed anger to guide my responses. This experience was a turning point, illustrating the transformative power of emotional intelligence. It was then that I realized the potential of EQ and embarked on a journey to enhance my own emotional intelligence.

In this book, we'll embark on a journey to explore the foundational aspects of emotional intelligence, understand its components, and recognize its profound impact on our lives. Each chapter is meticulously designed to build on the previous one, incorporating practical exercises, real-life examples, and self-assessment tools. These tools are theoretical concepts and practical instruments that will empower you to grow. Whether managing workplace dynamics, improving family ties, or enhancing romantic relationships, the strategies here are tailored to foster understanding and lend themselves to practical application.

After years of studying the nuances of EQ, I am thrilled to help you enhance your emotional skills. This book is not just an exploration of theories but a practical guide to making significant life changes.

The goal here is crystal clear—to equip you with the knowledge and tools necessary to transform your emotional intelligence into a driving force for success and fulfillment in all areas of your life. This journey requires an open mind and a commitment to self-discovery, but I assure you, the rewards are not just promising but life-changing. Your effort will be rewarded with a richer, more rewarding personal and professional existence.

So, let's get started. Embrace this opportunity to unlock your full potential through the power of Emotional Intelligence. By the end of this book, you'll understand what makes EQ so vital and how to actively improve and apply it in every part of your life, ensuring a richer, more rewarding personal and professional existence.

CHAPTER 1
FOUNDATIONS OF EMOTIONAL INTELLIGENCE

Have you ever encountered someone who excels in their career and maintains thriving relationships despite having an average IQ? What sets them apart is a more elusive skill set centered around emotional intelligence. This chapter will unravel the intricate layers of EQ, debunk common myths, and illuminate how this powerful tool can be actively developed through understanding its scientific roots and evolutionary path.

THE SCIENCE BEHIND EMOTIONAL INTELLIGENCE: DEBUNKING MYTHS

Emotional Intelligence Is Innate: A Common Misconception

While some individuals might seem naturally adept at navigating social situations or managing their emotions, the belief that emotional intelligence is purely an innate trait is a misconception. Like any other skill, Emotional intelligence can be honed and developed over time. This development is rooted in the brain's extraordinary capacity to adapt and rewire itself—a concept known as neuroplasticity. Just as a musician practices an instrument to improve their skill, you can train your brain to enhance your emotional capabilities. The implication here is profound—every person has the potential to elevate their emotional intelligence through conscious effort and training. By engaging in targeted exercises like mindfulness or reflective journaling, you actively forge new neural pathways that bolster your emotional faculties.

The Brain's Plasticity: Shaping Emotional Intelligence

Neuroplasticity is the brain's ability to reorganize itself by forming new neural connections throughout life. This ability allows the skills associated with EQ—such as empathy, self-regulation, and motivation—to be cultivated at any stage. When you learn new emotional skills, your brain builds and strengthens networks that make these skills more accessible and practical. For instance, practicing empathy can enhance the neural pathways that help you understand and share the feelings of others, essentially training your brain to be more empathetic. This scientific understanding lets you know that change is possible and can physically manifest within your brain's architecture.

Myth versus Reality: Clarifying Misunderstandings about EQ

One of the most persistent myths about emotional intelligence is that EQ is less important than IQ. EQ is often a stronger predictor of personal and professional success than IQ. Emotional intelligence helps you navigate the social complexities of the workplace, lead and motivate others, and excel in your career—achievements that raw intelligence alone cannot facilitate. Furthermore, EQ plays a critical role in personal relationships, affecting everything from choosing a partner to maintaining deep, satisfying connections.

Understanding the tangible benefits of emotional intelligence can motivate you to invest in developing this crucial skill set.

The Evolution of EQ: Tracing its Development

The understanding of emotional intelligence has evolved significantly since it first emerged as a psychological theory in the 1960s. Initially, the focus was primarily on recognizing one's own emotions and those of others. Over the decades, this concept has expanded to encompass a broader range of skills, including emotional regulation and the ability to use emotional information to guide thinking and behavior. Today, emotional intelligence is recognized as a set of personal capabilities and a pivotal factor influencing a wide array of societal dynamics, including leadership, team performance, and interpersonal relationships. Understanding this evolution helps contextualize why EQ is a valued asset today, reinforcing the importance of actively developing these skills.

MEASURING YOUR EMOTIONAL QUOTIENT: THE FIRST STEP TO GROWTH

Understanding the nuances of emotional intelligence begins with an accurate measure of where you currently stand, much like a doctor would assess a patient before treatment. EQ tests serve this purpose, providing a snapshot of your emotional competencies and areas with room for enhancement. However, it's important to note that these tests are not the be-all and end-all of your emotional capabilities. Instead, they are a starting point—a diagnostic tool that helps you identify strengths and weaknesses in your emotional functioning. These assessments vary widely, from structured interviews and self-report questionnaires to 360-degree feedback forms where individuals receive evaluations from peers, supervisors, and direct reports. Each type of test has its focus, whether measuring your ability to perceive emotions accurately, understand emotional states, manage emotions within yourself, or handle interpersonal relationships effectively.

Despite their usefulness, EQ tests have their limitations. They often rely on self-perception, which can be biased or inaccurate. For example, you may rate your ability to manage stress as high because you don't typically feel overwhelmed, not realizing that you unconsciously deflect stress onto others around you. Therefore, while these tests provide valuable insights, they should be seen as part of a more extensive process of emotional growth, not a definitive grading of your emotional skills. To truly benefit from an EQ assessment, it's crucial to approach the results with an open mind and a readiness to explore deeper self-understanding rather than as a judgment of character or ability.

Emotional Intelligence Self-Assessment Test

For each statement, choose the response that best describes you. Use the following scale:

1. Strongly Disagree
2. Disagree
3. Neutral
4. Agree
5. Strongly Agree

Self-Awareness

1. I understand why I feel the way I do in different situations.
2. I can recognize my emotions as I experience them.
3. I am aware of how my emotions affect my thoughts and behaviors.

Self-Regulation

4. I stay calm under pressure.
5. I am good at controlling my impulses.
6. I manage my emotions well, even in difficult situations.

Motivation

7. I set goals and work diligently to achieve them.
8. I stay motivated even when faced with setbacks.
9. I enjoy challenges and am willing to take risks to achieve my goals.

Empathy

10. I am good at understanding how others are feeling.
11. I listen attentively to what others are saying.
12. I can sense when someone is upset, even if they haven't said anything.

Social Skills

13. I find it easy to make new friends.
14. I handle conflict with others effectively.
15. I am good at building and maintaining relationships.

Scoring:

Add up your scores for each pillar. Each pillar has a maximum score of fifteen.

- Self-Awareness: Questions 1-3
- Self-Regulation: Questions 4-6
- Motivation: Questions 7-9
- Empathy: Questions 10-12
- Social Skills: Questions 13-15

Interpreting Your Scores

- 13-15: Strong skills in this area
- 10-12: Good skills but room for improvement
- 7-9: Moderate skills; consider working on this area
- 3-6: Low skills; significant improvement needed

Use this test as a tool to understand your current emotional intelligence levels. Reflect on your scores and identify areas where you'd like to grow. Remember, the journey to emotional intelligence is ongoing, and each step you take brings you closer to unlocking your full potential!

Moving forward from testing, the deployment of various self-assessment tools is instrumental. These tools range from simple journal prompts that encourage you to reflect on daily emotional experiences to more structured diaries where you record and analyze specific emotional reactions and the situations that trigger them. Apps and online platforms offer interactive assessments that track your emotional responses over time, providing analysis and feedback to help you understand patterns in your emotional behavior. If you use an iPhone, Apple's new app, Journal, is a great tool to start using. These tools serve as mirrors, reflecting your emotional habits and tendencies, and they are most effective when used regularly over a period of time. By consistently monitoring your emotions and the contexts in which they arise, you develop a sharper awareness of your emotional triggers and better strategies for managing them.

Interpreting the results from EQ assessments and self-monitoring tools is another critical step. This is not about assigning a score but understanding what your emotional responses say about you. For instance, if you consistently rate low on empathy, it might suggest a need to work on understanding and sharing the feelings of others more effectively. Conversely, high scores in self-regulation indicate a strong ability to control impulses and remain calm under pressure. Each piece of data provides insight into your emotional functioning and outlines a path for personal development. This interpretation guides your growth, helping you identify specific areas where targeted efforts can substantially improve how you relate to yourself and others.

Lastly, the importance of setting baselines must be considered. These initial measurements of your EQ serve as benchmarks for tracking your progress. Just as a long-distance runner keeps track of race times to gauge improvement, regularly assessing your emotional intelligence helps you see where you need to improve and how far you've come. This tracking isn't just concerned with noting better scores or fewer emotional mishaps; it's about recognizing the deeper integration of emotional intelligence into your daily life. As you become more adept at handling emotional challenges, you'll find that situations that once triggered a cascade of negativity now provoke a more measured, thoughtful response. This evolution, observable through periodic reassessment against your baseline, is the most compelling testament to the power of dedicated effort in cultivating your emotional intelligence.

THE FIVE COMPONENTS OF EQ EXPLAINED

Self-Awareness: Understanding Oneself through Emotional Intelligence

Self-awareness, the cornerstone of emotional intelligence, involves an acute understanding of one's emotions, strengths, weaknesses, and drives. It means recognizing how your feelings affect others and your interactions with the world. A person with high self-awareness understands where their feelings come from and how they can impact their thoughts and actions. This awareness is crucial because it forms the basis of all other EQ skills. For example, consider a scenario in which a manager receives critical feedback from a superior. An individual with solid self-awareness will recognize their initial feelings of defensiveness but also understand the underlying reasons for these emotions, perhaps recognizing a fear of inadequacy or a dislike of criticism. This understanding allows them to process their feelings more constructively, preventing a knee-jerk reaction that could damage relationships or hinder personal growth.

Moreover, self-awareness extends to recognizing how your emotional state can influence your decision-making and behavior. It means understanding your emotional triggers and predicting how you will react in different situations. This insight is invaluable in personal relationships and professional settings where strategic thinking and interpersonal relationships are key. For instance, if you know that you are prone to stress under tight deadlines, you can implement strategies in advance to mitigate stress, such as planning your tasks more meticulously or delegating when possible.

Self-Regulation: Managing Emotions for Better Outcomes

Self-regulation refers to controlling or redirecting disruptive emotions and impulses and adapting to changing circumstances. It means not getting overly angry or upset or behaving impulsively. Effective self-regulation involves the capacity to think before acting and the power to express oneself appropriately. Strategies for enhancing self-regulation include mindfulness practices, which encourage staying present and aware, thus allowing for more deliberate actions and responses. Another powerful method is cognitive reappraisal, which involves changing the emotional response to a situation by reinterpreting its meaning. For example, instead of viewing a challenging work project as a potential for failure, see it as an opportunity to learn and grow, thereby reducing anxiety and improving your focus.

Self-regulation also involves staying calm and clear-headed under pressure. This aspect of EQ is particularly valuable in crises where emotional overreactions can exacerbate problems. Maintaining control over your emotions allows you to make more rational decisions, not clouded by fear, anger, or frustration. Consider a situation where a project you lead goes differently than planned. A regulated response would involve the following:

- Assessing the situation calmly.
- Gathering facts.
- Making reasoned decisions about the best steps forward rather than panicking or placing blame.

Motivation: The Internal Drive That Propels Us Forward

In the context of EQ, motivation is predominantly intrinsic—it comes from within rather than being driven by external rewards like money or fame. It involves pursuing goals with energy and persistence. High motivation levels lead individuals to be highly productive and effective in whatever they undertake. This component of emotional intelligence is about aligning your deeper personal values with your day-to-day actions and goals. For instance, if you value community service, you may find motivation in roles that allow you to help others and give back, regardless of the financial remuneration.

Motivation sustains us through challenges and setbacks. It helps us initiate, guide, and maintain goal-oriented behaviors crucial in personal and professional realms. To foster your intrinsic motivation, set goals that are personally meaningful and interesting to you and ensure that these goals are attainable yet challenging enough to engage your skills and passions.

Empathy: Connecting with Others on a Deeper Level

Empathy, another central component of EQ, involves understanding other people's emotional makeup. It concerns more than just recognizing how others are feeling; it's also about acknowledging and appreciating their emotions. Empathy promotes tolerance and helps you develop more profound, more connected relationships. It allows for an emotional connection transcending simple day-to-day interactions, facilitating deeper bonds and a greater understanding of others.

Empathy can look like a leader who notices that one of their team members seems unusually quiet and withdrawn and takes the time to ask if everything is okay, thereby providing support. Or it could be a friend who recognizes the excitement behind your words when you talk about a new hobby and encourages you to pursue it. Each of these instances strengthens relationships and enhances social interactions, which are crucial for personal and professional success.

Social Skills: Navigating the Social Landscape Effectively

Finally, social skills in emotional intelligence encompass a range of competencies, including effective communication, the ability to persuade, leadership qualities, and conflict resolution skills. These skills enable people to interact well with others, building rapport and forming alliances. They are vital in managing relationships, networking, and building bonds based on mutual trust and respect.

Effective communication, for example, involves speaking clearly or persuasively, actively listening, and appropriately responding to others' verbal and nonverbal signals. High EQ can help de-escalate tensions and promote understanding and compromise in conflict situations. For instance, during a disagreement, an emotionally intelligent person would remain receptive to the other person's perspective and express their viewpoint non-aggressively but rather cooperatively, seeking a solution that benefits all parties involved.

By developing these five components of emotional intelligence, you equip yourself with a toolkit that enhances your interactions and amplifies your professional capabilities, allowing for a more fulfilling and successful life.

EMOTIONAL INTELLIGENCE VERSUS IQ: WHY EQ MATTERS MORE IN RELATIONSHIPS

Complementing IQ with EQ: Balancing Cognitive and Emotional Skills

While the traditional measure of intelligence quotient (IQ) has long been valued as a predictor of academic and professional success, its role in personal fulfillment and interpersonal relationships is considerably limited. IQ tests measure specific abilities, including mathematical skill, logical reasoning, and linguistic prowess; however, they fall short in assessing qualities such as empathy, self-awareness, and the capacity to manage one's emotions and understand those of others. This is where emotional intelligence plays a crucial role, complementing IQ by filling in the emotional and relational aspects that IQ does not address.

Imagine two professionals in a meeting, one with a high IQ but average EQ and another with a high EQ but average IQ. While the first might excel in analyzing data and generating reports, they might need help to lead a team effectively, motivate colleagues, or resolve conflicts. With a firm grasp of emotional dynamics, the second individual might excel in negotiating deals, fostering team cohesion, or managing crises. Both types of intelligence quotient are essential, but EQ is often the more critical in many real-world scenarios, especially when navigating complex social situations and maintaining solid relationships.

The synergy between IQ and EQ is particularly evident in scenarios requiring a holistic problem-solving and decision-making approach. For instance, a doctor with a high IQ can diagnose diseases accurately in healthcare. Still, without a high EQ, they may struggle to communicate effectively with patients or empathize with their concerns, which can be crucial for treatment adherence and patient satisfaction. Thus, while IQ provides foundational knowledge and analytical ability, EQ enhances it by adding a human element to the skills often necessary for success in both personal and professional realms.

EQ in Personal Relationships: Fostering Deeper Connections

In personal relationships, EQ is a formidable predictor of success and satisfaction. Whether familial, romantic, or platonic, relationships require high emotional engagement—understanding, patience, and empathy—not captured by IQ. Emotional intelligence facilitates more profound connections with others by emphasizing recognition and management of one's emotions and understanding those of others.

Consider the dynamics of a romantic relationship, where conflicts are inevitable. A partner with high EQ will probably handle disagreements with more empathy and awareness, focusing on communication and mutual understanding rather than winning the argument. They are adept at reading nonverbal cues, understanding their partner's emotional state, and responding appropriately. This capability helps resolve the issue amicably and strengthens the relationship by reinforcing a foundation of trust and understanding.

Moreover, EQ is crucial in parenting. A parent with high emotional intelligence can better understand the needs and emotions of their children, regardless of the child's age. This understanding is vital in providing support, guidance, and nurture, significantly influencing a child's emotional and psychological development. Thus, in the intimate weave of personal relationships, EQ acts as a critical tool for building and maintaining bonds that are fulfilling and resilient in the face of challenges.

EQ in the Workplace: Enhancing Leadership and Collaboration

Emotional Intelligence is increasingly recognized as a driver of success in professional settings, particularly in leadership roles. Leaders with high EQ can inspire and motivate their teams, manage stress and conflict, and maintain positive workplace relationships. These leaders understand that emotions can drive behavior and influence the workplace climate. They are skilled in managing both their own emotions and those of others to maintain productivity and morale.

An emotionally intelligent leader also recognizes team members' strengths and weaknesses, allows for effective task delegation and conflict resolution, and fosters a supportive work environment. This skill set is essential in today's diverse workplace, where cultural sensitivities and varied communication styles require nuanced understanding and management. For example, during organizational changes, which can be a source of significant stress and uncertainty, a leader with high EQ can navigate the transition smoothly by addressing concerns empathetically and transparently, thereby maintaining trust and stability within the team.

The Limitations of IQ: Understanding Its Role and Boundaries

While IQ is undoubtedly important in domains that require high cognitive effort, its limitations become apparent when predicting overall life success and happiness. IQ tests do not measure creativity, leadership, empathy, or resilience—traits increasingly recognized as integral to navigating the complexities of modern life. High IQ can contribute to academic and professional success, but without the balancing effect of EQ, it may lead to unfulfilled relationships and ineffective leadership.

The added value of high EQ cannot be overstated, especially in an era where automation and artificial intelligence make purely cognitive capabilities less of a uniquely human trait. In contrast, the qualities measured by EQ represent distinctly human skills that machines are unlikely to replicate fully. Therefore, developing EQ is not just about complementing IQ but investing in capabilities that enhance interpersonal relations and adaptability in a rapidly changing world.

Understanding the interplay between IQ and EQ reveals that while cognitive intelligence can open doors to opportunities, emotional intelligence builds and enriches the relationships that make those opportunities worthwhile. This blend of knowing and feeling, analyzing and empathizing, forms the bedrock of personal satisfaction and lasting success in all areas of life.

CHAPTER 2
SELF-AWARENESS MASTERY

In the labyrinth of human emotions, understanding ourselves is often as challenging as navigating complex social networks or mastering professional skills. Yet, self-awareness stands as the cornerstone of emotional intelligence, pivotal in transforming how you perceive yourself and how you interact with the world around you. Imagine embarking on a voyage across uncharted waters without a map; similarly, navigating life's emotional tides can seem daunting without self-awareness. This chapter delves into recognizing and managing your emotional triggers, a fundamental skill for anyone looking to enhance their EQ and lead a more balanced, harmonious life.

IDENTIFYING YOUR EMOTIONAL TRIGGERS

Recognizing Triggers

The first step in mastering self-awareness is to recognize the external events or internal thoughts that trigger strong emotional responses in you. These triggers can vary widely among individuals, including a stressful work environment, criticism from others, or personal fears such as failure or rejection. Understanding these triggers is like uncovering hidden tripwires, which, once exposed, can be navigated with greater ease. To identify your emotional triggers, observe situations in which you feel powerful emotions. What were you doing? Who were you with? What thoughts were crossing your mind? This initial awareness creates a foundation for deeper exploration and managing your emotional landscape.

Journaling for Awareness

An effective tool in this quest for self-understanding is journaling. By keeping a daily record of your thoughts and feelings, you can capture the moments that cause emotional spikes and the subtler, day-to-day variations in your mood. Journaling acts as a mirror, reflecting your emotional patterns and triggers back to you, thus facilitating a deeper understanding of your emotional self. When journaling, focus on being as honest and detailed as possible. Describe your emotions, rate their intensity, and note any potential triggers. Over time, this practice can offer profound insights into how your emotions operate and what provokes them, paving the way for more controlled and mindful responses.

Patterns of Reaction

As you journal and observe your emotional reactions, patterns will inevitably emerge. Perhaps you'll notice that your anxiety spikes during meetings with a particular colleague or that you feel irritable after scrolling through social media. Recognizing these patterns is essential, as it helps predict future emotional responses and empowers you to take proactive steps in managing them. For instance, if you identify that lack of sleep contributes to next-day irritability, you can prioritize better sleep habits to mitigate this response. Understanding your reaction patterns enables you to not only react to emotional triggers but also anticipate and manage them effectively.

The Role of Past Experiences

It's important to acknowledge that our emotional triggers are often rooted in past experiences. A fear of public speaking might stem from a childhood incident of being laughed at during a school performance. Understanding the origin of your emotional responses can be illuminating and freeing. This awareness allows you to contextualize your feelings and, if necessary, work through the lingering effects of past traumas with a therapist or counselor. Recognizing that your reactions do not just relate to the present moment but also relate to echoes from the past can be a powerful tool in your emotional toolkit, helping you to respond to current triggers more thoughtfully and less reactively.

By embracing these strategies, you can begin to untangle the web of your emotions, turning what once might have seemed like overwhelming reactions into manageable, understandable aspects of your psyche. This process is not just about control but about integration and acceptance, leading to a more emotionally intelligent, responsive, and harmonious existence.

THE POWER OF JOURNALING FOR EMOTIONAL INSIGHT

Often seen as a simple diary entry, journaling can be a profound tool for gaining deep emotional insight. This process allows you to articulate thoughts and feelings that may be too complex or fleeting to understand in the moment. When considering the approach to journaling, you'll find that both structured and free-form methods offer unique benefits. Structured journaling typically involves prompts or guided questions that direct your reflection on specific topics or incidents. This can be particularly helpful when you're new to journaling or feel overwhelmed by where to start. It provides a framework that can lead to insights you might not have explored otherwise. For example, a structured prompt such as, "What were three high and low emotional points of your day?" can guide you to reflect on daily fluctuations in your mood that you might otherwise overlook.

On the other hand, free-form journaling is more like a stream of consciousness, where you write whatever comes to mind without any specific direction or constraints. This method can be incredibly liberating for those confined by structure and seeking a more organic way to express their thoughts and feelings. The lack of guidelines encourages an accessible exploration of thoughts, sometimes leading to unexpected connections or realizations. For instance, you may start by writing about a stressful incident at work and uncover a more profound, underlying anxiety about your career path that merits further exploration.

Both methods have their place in cultivating emotional intelligence, and your preference can change depending on your current emotional state or the specific insights you're seeking at the time. On some days, the structured approach may help you tackle a particular emotional challenge, while on other days, the free-form method could be more therapeutic, providing the space to vent and explore freely.

Reflective journaling practices are another layer of this explorative tool, focusing more on analyzing and making sense of the emotions and events you've journaled about. This practice can deepen your self-understanding by encouraging you to look back at your entries from a distance of days or weeks. This reflection can reveal how your emotions evolve and how your initial reactions to situations may change upon review. Reflective journaling acts as a mirror and a map; it shows you where you have been emotionally and helps you navigate where you may want to go in terms of emotional growth.

Tracking emotions is a vital aspect of journaling that can be particularly enlightening. By consistently noting how you feel across different situations, you begin to see patterns that may be affecting your emotional health. For instance, you might discover that your stress levels rise mid-week due to increased work demands or that you feel consistently low after interacting with a specific friend. These insights allow you to make more informed decisions about changes you may need to make, whether adjusting your workload, addressing relationship dynamics, or changing your routines. Tracking your emotions can also be instrumental in managing mental health, as it provides tangible data to be discussed with a therapist or counselor.

Finally, making journaling a regular habit is important for ongoing emotional growth. Consistency turns what could be a sporadic insight into a rich, continual understanding of your emotional life. To integrate journaling into your daily routine, start by setting a specific time each day for this practice. Whether it's first thing in the morning, during a lunch break, or right before bed, find a time to commit to writing for a few minutes. Keeping your journal accessible, perhaps on your bedside table or in your daily bag, removes barriers to journaling and reminds you of your commitment. Additionally, setting small, achievable goals, such as journaling for five minutes daily, can prevent overwhelming feelings and make the habit more straightforward to maintain. As the benefits of this practice begin to manifest—such as increased calmness, greater emotional resilience, and enhanced self-awareness—you'll likely find that journaling becomes an indispensable part of your emotional well-being toolkit.

USING MINDFULNESS TO ENHANCE SELF-AWARENESS

Mindfulness, often misconstrued as a mere trend, is a profound practice rooted in ancient traditions, now validated by modern psychology for its benefits in enhancing self-awareness and emotional intelligence. At its core, mindfulness involves maintaining a moment-by-moment awareness of our thoughts, feelings, bodily sensations, and surrounding environment with openness and non-judgment. This practice encourages you to observe your present experiences without criticism and to foster a greater awareness of your emotional and mental state. In the context of emotional intelligence, mindfulness serves as a critical tool, allowing you to engage with your feelings without becoming overwhelmed, thus providing a stable platform to understand and manage your emotions more effectively.

To incorporate mindfulness into your daily routine, you can begin with simple exercises. One effective technique is the practice of mindful breathing, where you focus solely on your breath, observing each inhalation and exhalation without trying to alter them. This can be done for just a few minutes at a time, perhaps at the beginning of your day or when you feel particularly stressed. Another accessible practice is the mindful observation of your environment, which involves picking a natural object within your immediate vicinity and focusing on watching it for a minute or two. This could be anything from a tree swaying in the wind, a cloud passing overhead, or even the rain falling against your window. The key is to observe the object and the details of its movement and existence, allowing your mind to become absorbed in the present moment, thereby easing away from distracting thoughts or emotional turbulence.

The connection between mindfulness and emotional intelligence is profound. By fostering an enhanced state of self-awareness, mindfulness allows you to better recognize your emotional patterns and triggers, a significant aspect of emotional intelligence. For instance, as you practice mindful breathing, you may notice that specific thoughts or environmental factors trigger anxiety or stress. With this awareness, you can work on addressing these triggers more constructively. Furthermore, mindfulness encourages a non-reactive form of emotional engagement. It teaches you to observe your feelings without immediately reacting, allowing you to choose how to respond. This ability to manage your responses is critical to emotional intelligence, particularly in challenging or high-stress situations where unguarded reactions can lead to regrettable outcomes.

However, embarking on a mindfulness practice is challenging, especially for beginners. Many individuals report difficulties such as becoming easily distracted, feeling impatient, or struggling with the silence that mindfulness often requires. It's common to become frustrated when you find your mind wandering continuously. It's vital to approach mindfulness with a sense of kindness toward yourself to overcome these challenges. Understand that distraction is a normal part of the learning process and that mindfulness, like any other skill, requires practice and patience to develop. Start with concise practices, perhaps just a minute or two of focused breathing or observation, and gradually increase the duration as you become more comfortable with the practice. Additionally, guided mindfulness exercises, found in numerous apps and online platforms, can provide direction and structure that help keep your practice on track.

By integrating mindfulness into your daily life and overcoming the initial hurdles of the practice, you can significantly enhance your emotional awareness and intelligence. This benefits your sense of well-being and improves your interactions and relationships with others as you become more attuned to your feelings and the emotional states of those around you. Mindfulness, therefore, is not just a self-contained practice but a gateway to a more emotionally intelligent, responsive, and fulfilling life.

FEEDBACK LOOPS: HOW TO USE THEM TO YOUR ADVANTAGE

Feedback loops are dynamic and instrumental in enhancing emotional intelligence, acting like a compass guiding sailors through uncharted waters. Simply put, a feedback loop in personal development involves receiving and processing feedback about one's behaviors and emotions and then applying that information to foster growth and change. This ongoing cycle can significantly amplify your self-awareness and adaptability, making it an indispensable tool in your EQ toolkit.

To effectively use feedback loops for emotional growth, it's important to actively seek out constructive feedback. This type of feedback should be purposeful and supportive, aimed at fostering improvement rather than merely pointing out faults. Consider reaching out to individuals whose opinions you trust—mentors, close friends, family members, or colleagues. These should be people who understand you well and can provide insights into how your emotional behaviors appear from an external perspective. When requesting feedback, be specific about the areas where you seek insights, such as handling conflict or managing stress. This specificity makes it easier for others to provide helpful feedback and helps you focus on key areas for your emotional growth.

Constructive feedback is only as valuable as your ability to receive and integrate it effectively. Feeling defensive or uncomfortable when faced with criticism is natural, but embracing vulnerability and openness to change is essential. When receiving feedback, listen actively without interrupting, ask clarifying questions if necessary, and reflect on the insights provided. It's important not to rush this process—allow yourself time to digest the information and consider its validity and applicability to your life. This reflective practice does not mean accepting all feedback as absolute truth but rather evaluating its relevance and utility in your growth journey.

In addition to external feedback, developing robust self-feedback mechanisms is vital. These mechanisms involve regularly reflecting on your emotional responses and behaviors and assessing them against your personal goals and values. Techniques such as self-reflection, which might involve revisiting situations that elicited strong emotional responses, and self-assessment, which could include periodic reviews of your emotional reactions over time, are helpful here. These practices encourage a deeper understanding of your emotional patterns and triggers, helping you recognize areas where you react well and others where you might benefit from different approaches.

Using feedback effectively is the most essential step in closing the feedback loop. This involves translating the insights gained from external feedback and self-reflection into actionable steps toward emotional growth. For example, suppose feedback highlights a tendency to become overly anxious during presentations. In that case, you may decide to work on strategies such as deep breathing or positive visualization to manage your anxiety. Equally, suppose self-assessment reveals that you are particularly adept at mediating conflicts. In that case, you might further strengthen this skill and consider roles or opportunities where this strength can be used.

Implementing changes based on feedback often requires setting specific, realistic goals and identifying the resources or support needed to achieve them. This could involve seeking further training, reading relevant materials, or engaging in reflective practices like journaling or mindfulness. The key is viewing feedback as a valuable resource for continuous learning and self-improvement rather than a critique or an endpoint.

Feedback loops, when effectively integrated into your personal development strategy, can dramatically enhance your emotional intelligence by providing continuous insights and opportunities for growth. These loops encourage a proactive approach to managing and improving your emotional skills, ensuring you remain responsive and adaptable in an ever-changing environment. As you continue to engage in this iterative process of feedback and growth, you'll likely find that your emotional intelligence and self-awareness improve, and your relationships and professional life will also benefit.

As we conclude this chapter, remember that mastering self-awareness through identifying triggers, journaling, mindfulness, and feedback loops sets a solid foundation for more advanced emotional intelligence skills. These practices are essential stepping stones, preparing you for the deeper exploration of empathy, motivation, and social skills that will be covered in the upcoming chapters. Each step builds upon the last, forming a ladder leading to heightened emotional intelligence and, ultimately, a more fulfilling and successful life.

CHAPTER 3
MANAGING YOUR EMOTIONS

In the ever-changing tides of our daily lives, where each moment can bring challenges and surprises, learning to manage our emotions is nothing short of navigating a ship through stormy seas. Maintaining emotional equilibrium is crucial for personal peace and engaging effectively with the world around us. This chapter focuses on developing robust strategies for emotional regulation, ensuring you can face both high waves and calm waters with equal composure. Here, we delve into practical techniques and personalized plans that aid in managing overwhelming emotions, empowering you to steer your emotional journey with confidence and self-compassion.

STRATEGIES FOR COOLING DOWN WHEN YOU'RE OVERWHELMED

Breathing Techniques: A Gateway to Calm

When overwhelmed, one of your most immediate and effective tools is your breath. Breathing techniques are a cornerstone of emotional regulation, offering a quick and powerful means to influence your body's stress response and restore a sense of calm. One effective method is deep belly breathing, which involves deep, even inhalations through your nose, allowing your abdomen to rise, followed by slow, controlled exhalations through your mouth. This technique stimulates the parasympathetic nervous system—often called the "rest and digest" system—which helps mitigate the "fight or flight" response triggered by stress.

Another helpful technique is the 4-7-8 breathing method, developed by Dr. Andrew Weil. This involves breathing in for a count of four, holding the breath for a count of seven, and exhaling for a count of eight. This method helps reduce anxiety and aids in sleep, making it particularly beneficial during times of stress. Integrating these breathing exercises into your daily routine, especially during moments of calm, can prepare you to deploy them more effectively when overwhelmed, turning them into a reflexive response to stress.

Physical versus Emotional Responses: Understanding and Managing Each

Stress and overwhelming emotions often manifest through physical and emotional symptoms, influencing the other. Physically, you may experience increased heart rate, sweating, or a tense feeling in your stomach. Emotionally, stress can lead to irritability, anxiety, or a sense of being out of control. Distinguishing between these responses is crucial for effective management.

For physical symptoms, techniques like progressive muscle relaxation, where you tense and then relax different muscle groups, can be beneficial. This helps alleviate bodily tension and has a calming effect on the mind. Cognitive behavioral techniques such as reframing negative thoughts can be effective for emotional symptoms. This involves consciously changing your perspective on stressful situations, focusing on potential positive outcomes or aspects rather than dwelling on the negatives. This cognitive shift can significantly alter your emotional response, helping you maintain a balanced outlook even in stressful situations.

Creating a Personal Calm-Down Plan: Tailored Strategies for Emotional Regulation

A personalized calm-down plan is like having a tailored map that guides you back to an emotional equilibrium whenever you find yourself lost in the sea of overwhelming feelings. This plan identifies strategies that work best in stressful situations, including specific breathing techniques, listening to calming music, practicing mindfulness, or engaging in physical activities like walking or yoga.

Identify activities that naturally bring you peace and integrate them into your plan. Next, consider the environments where you feel most relaxed—perhaps nature, a particular room in your home, or a favorite café—and think about how to access these spaces when you feel overwhelmed. Also, include people who calm you, whether through their presence or conversation and consider how you can reach out to them during difficult times. With this plan in place, you empower yourself with tools and strategies to deploy when emotions run high, ensuring you can navigate back to calm waters more efficiently.

The Importance of Self-Compassion in Emotional Regulation

The role of self-compassion in managing overwhelming emotions cannot be overstated. Being kind to yourself is not just about comfort—it's a strategic approach that enhances your resilience to stress. Self-compassion involves treating yourself with the same kindness and understanding during tough times that you would offer a good friend. This approach helps soften the often harsh self-criticism that can accompany mistakes or difficult situations.

Practicing self-compassion can involve simple affirmations reinforcing your worth and humanity or more structured practices like mindfulness meditation focused on self-compassion. These practices help you accept your feelings without judgment, facilitating smoother emotional processing and quicker recovery from stress. By cultivating self-compassion, you not only soothe your current state but also build a stronger foundation for handling future stressors, reinforcing your emotional resilience.

Incorporating these strategies into your daily life prepares you to face overwhelming emotions when they arise and to move through them with greater ease and understanding. As you practice and refine these techniques, you'll find that managing your emotions becomes less about control and more about harmonious integration, ultimately leading to a more balanced and fulfilling life.

THE ROLE OF PHYSICAL EXERCISE IN EMOTIONAL REGULATION

Understanding the interplay between physical exercise and emotional regulation can significantly enhance your ability to manage stress and maintain mental health. Numerous studies have illuminated the science behind how engaging in regular physical activity can profoundly affect our brain chemistry, leading to improved mood and decreased feelings of anxiety and depression. At the core of this relationship is the release of endorphins, often called the body's natural painkillers, which elevate mood and create a sense of well-being. Additionally, exercise stimulates the production of neurotransmitters like serotonin and dopamine, which play crucial roles in mood regulation and cognitive function.

Physical exercise also contributes to better stress management by reducing levels of the body's stress hormones, such as adrenaline and cortisol. Over time, regular physical activity retrains the nervous system to handle stress more efficiently, a process called "neurological feedback." This means that individuals who exercise regularly are likely to experience less physiological reactivity during stress, which includes a lower heart rate and blood pressure response when faced with high-stress situations. This reduced reactivity not only helps at the moment but also decreases the time it takes to recover from stress, enhancing overall emotional resilience.

Moreover, regular physical activity improves sleep, often disrupted by stress and emotional upheaval. Good quality sleep is essential for emotional and psychological well-being as it helps the brain process emotional information. During sleep, the brain evaluates and remembers thoughts and memories, and poor sleep is closely linked to impaired mood and emotional reactivity. Improving sleep through exercise effectively supports your brain's ability to manage emotions and cope with stress more effectively.

Types of exercise that are particularly beneficial for emotional health include aerobic activities like jogging, swimming, cycling, and walking, as these stimulate neurotransmitter release and are generally accessible to most people. Yoga and Pilates can also be highly beneficial, as they combine physical movement with breathing techniques and mental focus, which are excellent for stress relief and emotional balance. Strength training, too, has been shown to improve mood and reduce symptoms of anxiety and depression, possibly due to the sense of accomplishment and increased self-esteem that often accompanies this type of training.

Integrating exercise into your daily routine can be a manageable task. Start small by incorporating more physical activity into your day-to-day life in simple ways—take the stairs instead of the elevator, go for a walk during your lunch break, or try a short home workout in the morning or evening. Setting realistic goals, such as a thirty-minute walk five days a week, can help make the practice more manageable and less overwhelming. Choosing activities you enjoy is also helpful, as you're more likely to stick with them long-term.

Another effective strategy is to link your exercise routine to existing habits, known as "habit stacking." For instance, if you drink coffee every morning, take a quick walk right after your coffee. This not only makes it easier to remember to exercise but also helps to establish a solid routine. Tracking your progress through a fitness app or a simple journal can provide motivation and a sense of accomplishment, encouraging regular exercise.

Regular physical activity is not just about improving physical health—it's vital to maintaining and enhancing emotional health. By incorporating regular, enjoyable physical activities into your lifestyle, you invest in a healthier body and a more resilient and balanced emotional life. This proactive approach to emotional regulation through exercise is a foundational strategy for building an active, emotionally enriched, and stable life.

CREATING YOUR EMOTIONAL EMERGENCY KIT

In the dynamic landscape of our emotional lives, moments of overwhelming stress and anxiety are inevitable. Just as you might keep a first aid kit for unexpected physical injuries, an emotional emergency kit can be your go-to resource for moments of emotional distress, providing immediate relief and comfort. I originally wasn't going to include this section in my book. But my wife, who suffers from occasional bouts of anxiety, carries with her an emergency kit of different essential oils to smell or rub on her wrist. This practice soothes her, and she swears by it. She told me I must include this section as it might help others like her. This kit should consist of various tools and soothing items you can turn to, ensuring immediate access to emotional first aid when needed. Among the essentials, consider including calming scents, such as lavender or chamomile, which can significantly alleviate stress through the power of aromatherapy. Research suggests that certain scents can trigger positive emotional responses from the brain, reducing cortisol levels and enhancing your sense of calm. Similarly, a playlist of comforting music that resonates with your emotions can be a therapeutic tool, harnessing music's profound impact on the brain's emotional and sensory pathways. Additionally, a collection of positive affirmations, carefully crafted and personalized to counteract your specific fears and anxieties, can help reorient your mind toward positive thinking during moments of doubt or panic.

Creating an emotional emergency kit that suits your unique emotional landscape is important. Personalization is vital because the effectiveness of each component depends on its resonance with your personal experiences and preferences. Start by reflecting on past instances when you felt overwhelmed and consider what brought you solace or relief. Was it a particular scent, a piece of music, or maybe a comforting texture or taste? Include these in your kit. Consider adding a comforting tactile object, like a soft blanket or a stress ball, which can help ground your senses and pull you away from spiraling negative thoughts. Holding or touching something comforting can be incredibly grounding and is a physical action that helps distract from emotional pain, providing a momentary refuge as you regroup emotionally.

The functionality of your emotional emergency kit extends to how and when to use it effectively. This kit is designed to be both a proactive and reactive tool. Proactively, you might use elements of your kit as part of your daily relaxation routines to maintain a baseline of reduced stress, which could include listening to your calming playlist during your commute or enjoying the scent of essential oils during evening downtime. Reactively, turn to your kit when you notice the early signs of emotional distress. Recognize the symptoms that precede your overwhelming emotions—perhaps increased heart rate, restlessness, or irritability—and promptly engage with your kit. For instance, if you start to feel anxious, you could step away to breathe in your calming scent or repeat a series of affirmations to challenge and control negative thoughts. The key is using these tools before your emotions escalate beyond manageable, averting a more profound emotional crisis.

An emotional emergency kit is beneficial for personal use and as a shared idea among friends and family. Encouraging loved ones to assemble their kits helps them manage their emotional health and fosters a shared understanding and support system within your community. Discussing what items each person has included in their kits and why can provide insights into personal coping mechanisms and emotional needs, enhancing empathy and support within the group. This shared approach normalizes the conversation around managing emotional health and strengthens communal bonds through mutual care and understanding. Sharing strategies and items that work for you may inspire others to adopt or adapt them, potentially providing new tools for someone else's kit and vice versa. This collective approach to emotional well-being creates an environment where members feel understood and supported, knowing they have the personal and communal resources to manage emotional challenges effectively.

NAVIGATING EMOTIONAL HIGHS AND LOWS WITH GRACE

Emotional variability is as natural as the changing tides in daily life. Accepting and navigating these shifts is crucial for a balanced and fulfilling life. Emotions can surge like high tides, bringing joy and exhilaration, or they can ebb to low points where sadness or melancholy might prevail. Both states hold intrinsic value, and learning to manage them effectively can enhance resilience and emotional agility.

Firstly, accepting emotional variability involves acknowledging that emotions are transient and do not define your character or capabilities. Recognizing that it's perfectly normal to feel ecstatic one moment and subdued the next can liberate you from self-judgment and allow you to experience life more fully. This acceptance is the first step toward using your emotional states to your advantage rather than being led by them.

When experiencing high emotionality, such as excitement or joy, it's important to savor these feelings while maintaining a grounding connection to your core self. Techniques such as grounding can be particularly effective here. This could involve physical actions like feeling the texture of the ground under your feet or mental practices like reminding yourself of your deeper values and long-term goals. These methods help prevent getting swept away by the high waves of immediate emotions. Additionally, channeling these high energies into creative or productive activities can be beneficial. Whether it's art, writing, or a physical endeavor like dance, using your elevated emotional states as a creative catalyst allows you to express these feelings and capture and transform them into something tangible.

Conversely, coping with lows requires a compassionate and nurturing approach. When faced with sadness or a lack of energy, techniques such as gentle self-talk can be a lifeline. Speak to yourself with kindness and understanding, acknowledging your feelings without pressure to quickly "snap out of it." Engaging in comforting and stimulating activities, such as reading a beloved book, watching a favorite show, or taking a warm bath, can also provide solace and a gentle way to recharge your emotional batteries. Mindfulness meditation can be particularly effective during these periods, as it encourages a non-judgmental awareness of your current state, helping to alleviate the weight of negative emotions.

Maintaining long-term emotional balance is akin to tending a garden; it requires regular care and attention. Regular self-reflection is a powerful tool in this ongoing process. By routinely examining your emotional experiences and reactions, you can gain insights into your emotional triggers and patterns, which can guide you in adjusting your lifestyle or thought processes to foster greater equilibrium. Integrating mindfulness into your daily routine can also play a significant role in sustaining balance. Daily meditation or mindful walking provides immediate relief from stress and strengthens your overall emotional resilience, making you better equipped to handle future emotional highs and lows.

These strategies for navigating the natural highs and lows of your emotional landscape are not just about coping mechanisms; they are about enriching your life experience, enhancing your self-awareness, and building a robust framework for emotional health. As you become more adept at riding these waves, you'll find that you can not only handle the challenges that come your way but also embrace life's joys and sorrows with equal grace and poise.

As we close this chapter, remember that embracing the full spectrum of your emotions with acceptance and awareness provides a pathway to deeper self-understanding and a more balanced life. These strategies are not just techniques to weather emotional storms but also ways to enhance your everyday living. As you move forward, each step you take in managing your emotions enriches your journey, preparing you for the complexities and joys of interpersonal relationships explored in the next chapter.

CHAPTER 4
MOTIVATION AND EMOTIONAL INTELLIGENCE

I magine you are an archer. Each arrow represents a goal, and your emotional intelligence fuels your bow. Drawing back the string requires understanding your emotional strengths and weaknesses, and releasing the arrow involves strategically directing your emotions to hit your target. This chapter will guide you in aligning your motivations with your emotional insights, transforming the art of goal setting into a more intuitive and effective process.

SETTING EQ-DRIVEN GOALS

Defining EQ-Driven Goals: Aligning Objectives with Emotional Insights

Setting EQ-driven goals involves a unique blend of self-awareness and forward-thinking, aligning your objectives with a deep understanding of your emotional capabilities and needs. These are not just goals; they reflect your values and the emotional strengths that resonate with your core identity. For instance, if empathy is one of your strong suits, you might aim to mentor a colleague or volunteer in community service. Alternatively, if self-regulation is an area where you excel, you may seek to lead a high-stakes project, knowing you can manage stress effectively.

The process begins by reflecting on your emotional patterns and triggers, which you've explored in previous chapters. Ask yourself: What are my emotional strengths? What situations bring out the best in me? What aspects of my emotional behavior could use improvement? Answers to these questions will help you formulate goals that are challenging, fulfilling, and tailored to leverage your emotional strengths, thereby increasing your chances of success.

The Role of Emotions in Goal Setting: Navigating Emotional Landscapes

Emotions play a pivotal role in setting and achieving goals. They can act both as powerful motivators and as barriers. For example, passion and excitement can propel you forward, infusing energy into your pursuits. At the same time, fear and doubt can create stumbling blocks that prevent you from even starting. Recognizing and managing these emotional drivers is crucial.

Consider the emotional landscape that surrounds your goals. If you aim to switch careers, acknowledge the fear of the unknown and the excitement of new opportunities. By addressing these emotions directly—perhaps through journaling or discussions with a mentor—you can devise strategies to bolster your courage and mitigate your fears. This emotional mapping clarifies what you're working toward and enhances your commitment to your goals.

SMART Goals and EQ: Crafting Goals with Emotional Intelligence

Integrating the SMART criteria—Specific, Measurable, Achievable, Relevant, and Time-bound—into your EQ-driven goals brings clarity and precision that aligns with emotional intelligence practices. For instance, if you aim to improve your empathy to enhance team collaboration, you may set a specific objective to conduct bi-weekly one-on-one meetings with team members. This goal is measurable by the number of meetings, achievable if you schedule them in advance, relevant to your broader aim of fostering team unity, and time-bound with a deadline to review progress at the end of the quarter.

Incorporating EQ into SMART goals means each element is infused with emotional understanding. A goal's relevance, for example, should resonate with your personal values and emotional needs, making it feel meaningful on a deeper level. This integration ensures that your goals are well-structured and deeply motivational.

Revisiting and Adjusting Goals: A Dynamic Process

As your emotional intelligence evolves, so too will your goals. The journey of emotional growth is ongoing, and your objectives need to reflect this dynamic process. Periodically revisiting your goals allows you to assess their relevance and feasibility in light of your current emotional state and capabilities. Perhaps you've discovered a newfound strength in handling complex negotiations, suggesting it's time to aim for more ambitious projects or roles that require this skill.

Setting regular intervals to review your goals, such as at the beginning of each new quarter, provides an opportunity to celebrate achievements, learn from setbacks, and realign your objectives with your current emotional landscape. This keeps you agile and responsive to changes in your emotional and professional life and ensures that your motivations remain strong and your goals are continually inspiring.

Navigating through this process, you will find that your goals are not just checkpoints but steps in a more extensive dance of emotional and personal development. They are both the path and the destination, each crafted and recalibrated to resonate with your deepest values and emotional insights, driving you forward in a continuous journey of growth and achievement.

THE RELATIONSHIP BETWEEN MOTIVATION AND EMOTIONAL STATE

Understanding the intricate dance between your emotional state and motivation can profoundly impact how you approach your goals and daily tasks. Emotions are powerful drivers that fuel your ambitions or hinder your progress. When you feel joyful or excited, tackling a challenging project or pursuing a long-term goal can seem invigorating and entirely achievable. Conversely, emotions like sadness or fear can dampen your enthusiasm and sap your energy, making even simple tasks feel daunting.

The first step in harnessing your emotions to boost motivation involves recognizing how different emotional states affect your drive. Positive emotions generally enhance motivation by broadening your sense of possibility and energizing your actions. For instance, when you feel happy, your brain is likely releasing dopamine, a neurotransmitter linked to the reward and pleasure centers, which not only makes you feel good but also reduces stress and increases focus, thereby enhancing productivity. On the other hand, emotions such as anxiety or frustration can lead to a decrease in dopamine levels, reducing your motivation and making you less inclined to pursue your goals.

To effectively leverage your emotions in boosting motivation, it's essential to identify your emotional motivators. These are specific feelings or emotional states that enhance your motivation. Some people might find that they're most motivated when they feel a sense of competition, while feelings of passion or curiosity might drive others. Reflect on times when you were highly motivated and note your emotions. Recognizing them can help you create conditions that replicate these feelings, enhancing your motivation when it starts to wane. For example, if you discover that curiosity is a strong motivator, you might structure your work to allow for exploration and learning, keeping your motivation high.

However, it's equally critical to address the impact of negative emotions on your motivation. Feelings of inadequacy, disappointment, or discouragement can undermine your drive to achieve your goals. To mitigate this effect, start by acknowledging these feelings rather than suppressing them. Understanding that it's normal to experience negative emotions can reduce their power over you. Techniques such as cognitive restructuring, which involves changing negative thought patterns into more positive, constructive ones, can be particularly effective here. For example, if you're feeling discouraged because you didn't reach a goal, instead of thinking, "I failed and am not good enough," you might reframe it to "I learned a lot from this experience and now have a better idea of how to succeed next time." Thomas Edison once said, "I have not failed. I've just found 10,000 ways that won't work," reminding us that each setback is simply a step toward discovering what truly succeeds.

Balancing your emotional states is crucial for maintaining optimal motivation. This doesn't mean seeking to feel happy all the time—such an expectation is both unrealistic and potentially unhelpful. Instead, aim for emotional agility, responding to changing emotional experiences with a mindful, productive attitude. One way to achieve this balance is through emotional journaling, where you regularly write about your feelings and the reasons for them, enhancing emotional regulation and clarity. Another effective strategy is engaging in activities that stabilize your mood, such as physical exercise, meditation, or hobbies that distract and soothe you. This approach helps maintain a level emotional landscape from which motivation can more easily spring.

By understanding and managing the relationship between your emotions and motivation, you equip yourself with the tools to maintain a steady drive toward your goals, regardless of the emotional ups and downs you may experience. This skill enhances your ability to achieve what you set out to do and contributes to a more satisfying and balanced approach to your personal and professional life.

OVERCOMING PROCRASTINATION THROUGH EMOTIONAL AWARENESS

Procrastination, often dismissed as laziness or poor time management, frequently has deeper emotional roots, such as fear of failure, anxiety, or perfectionism. These emotional factors can significantly hinder personal and professional progress, making tasks seem daunting or even unachievable. Understanding and addressing these emotional roots is important to overcoming procrastination and enhancing productivity.

Let's start by exploring the common emotional triggers of procrastination. Fear of failure is one of the most prevalent causes. This fear can paralyze you, creating a mental block where the prospect of not succeeding is so terrifying that not starting seems like a safer option. Similarly, perfectionism can lead to procrastination when the pressure to deliver flawless work becomes overwhelming, making it difficult to begin or proceed with a task. Anxiety, too, plays a role, particularly when it spirals into continued worries about the workload or potential outcomes, leading to a paralysis of analysis where you're stuck in planning without taking action.

Recognizing these emotional triggers is the first critical step toward managing procrastination. This awareness lets you understand that procrastination is not a character flaw but a response to underlying fears and anxieties. With this understanding, you can approach procrastination with more compassion and less judgment, which is essential in finding practical solutions. For instance, if fear of failure is at the heart of your procrastination, acknowledging this fear can be liberating. It lets you see that the real enemy is not the task but the fear itself. This realization opens up new avenues for tackling the task and the fear in manageable parts.

Addressing the emotional causes of procrastination involves several practical strategies that can transform your approach to work and deadlines. One effective method is to break down large tasks into smaller, more manageable steps. This technique reduces the overwhelm that can trigger procrastination, making the task less daunting and more achievable. For example, if writing a report feels overwhelming, break it down into stages such as research, outlining, writing the first draft, and revising. This makes the task more manageable and provides multiple opportunities for small successes along the way, boosting your confidence and motivation.

Another powerful strategy is to set clear, achievable deadlines for each small task rather than just one final deadline for the entire project. This approach creates a series of manageable goals and deadlines that can help maintain momentum and prevent the last-minute rush that often results from procrastination. It's also beneficial to schedule regular reviews of your progress. These check-ins can help you adjust your plan as needed, ensuring that you remain on track and can address any emerging issues before they lead to further delays.

Creating a supportive environment is also vital in combating procrastination. This involves both physical and social aspects. Physically, organize your workspace to minimize distractions. This might mean clearing clutter from your desk, using noise-canceling headphones, or setting boundaries with colleagues to ensure uninterrupted work time. Socially, seek support from peers or mentors who understand your goals and can offer encouragement and accountability. Knowing that someone else is aware of your deadlines and is rooting for your success can provide the extra push needed to get moving.

Additionally, consider the role of technology in creating a supportive environment. Various apps can help manage time effectively, block distracting websites, or provide platforms for tracking progress and setting reminders. Leveraging these tools can help you stay focused and organized, significantly reducing the tendency to procrastinate.

These strategies, rooted in a deep understanding of the emotional components of procrastination, offer a compassionate and effective approach to enhancing productivity. By recognizing and addressing the emotional triggers of procrastination, you can improve your work efficiency and develop greater emotional resilience, better preparing you for future challenges. As you implement these techniques, remember that overcoming procrastination does not mean pushing yourself harder but, instead, understanding yourself better and creating conditions that foster success and well-being.

EQ TECHNIQUES FOR SUSTAINING MOTIVATION

Maintaining a steady level of motivation can often feel like trying to keep a boat steady in choppy waters. Emotional balance is a critical component of this task, acting much like the keel of a ship, keeping it upright and on course despite the swirling currents. To achieve this emotional balance, several techniques can help smooth out the emotional peaks and troughs that might otherwise lead to motivational dips. One effective method is regular meditation, which helps cultivate a centered state of mind conducive to maintaining emotional equilibrium. Regular engagement in activities that inherently stabilize your mood, such as physical exercise or hobbies that you enjoy, can also contribute significantly to emotional balance. These activities provide a release valve for stress and build a routine that fosters a stable emotional environment, making it easier to sustain motivation over extended periods.

Incorporating positive affirmations into your daily routine is another powerful technique for enhancing self-esteem and motivation. Positive affirmations are statements you repeat to yourself to foster positive thinking and self-empowerment. For example, affirmations like "I am capable of achieving my goals" or "I embrace challenges as opportunities for growth" can reshape your mental landscape, reinforcing your self-worth and ability to overcome challenges. These affirmations act as mental armor, shielding you from the negative self-talk that can erode motivation and cloud your focus. By regularly affirming your strengths and capabilities, you create a self-fulfilling prophecy in which you believe in your ability to succeed and take action to ensure that success.

Visualizing success is another transformative technique that involves picturing a desired outcome or goal in your mind. This technique harnesses the power of your imagination to foster a positive mindset and align your emotions with your ambitions. When you visualize yourself achieving a goal, you engage the same neural networks that actual success would stimulate. This mental rehearsal primes your brain to act in ways that align with your vision, effectively programming your subconscious to recognize and seize opportunities that might otherwise go unnoticed. Visualization boosts your motivation by making your goals feel more attainable and enhances your emotional engagement with them, making the journey toward them more enjoyable and fulfilling.

Building resilience to setbacks is crucial for maintaining motivation in facing challenges. Resilience can be considered emotional buoyancy, the ability to stay afloat and keep moving forward even when the waters get rough. One way to build this resilience is through developing a growth mindset, which involves viewing failures and setbacks as opportunities to learn and grow rather than as insurmountable obstacles. This perspective encourages a proactive approach to challenges, where you actively seek lessons and avenues for improvement, thereby maintaining momentum. Another key aspect of building resilience is the practice of adaptive thinking, which involves adjusting your strategies and approaches in response to setbacks. This flexibility allows you to navigate difficulties more effectively, ensuring your motivation remains intact as you pivot and adapt to new circumstances.

As you integrate these techniques into your life, you'll find that sustaining motivation becomes less about exerting effort to push forward and more about maintaining a steady, balanced approach to your emotional and motivational landscape. This balanced approach enhances your ability to achieve your goals and makes the process more enjoyable and less stressful, contributing to a healthier, more productive life.

This chapter has explored various techniques to sustain motivation by maintaining emotional balance, using positive affirmations, visualizing success, and building resilience to setbacks. These strategies are designed to equip you with the tools necessary to navigate the emotional aspects of motivation, ensuring that you remain engaged and proactive in pursuing your goals. As we transition into the next chapter, we will delve deeper into empathy and its profound impact on personal and professional relationships. We will build on the foundation of emotional intelligence strategies discussed here to further enhance your interpersonal interactions and emotional well-being.

CHAPTER 5
EMPATHY—THE HEART OF CONNECTION

Imagine walking through a dense forest where each tree represents someone you've met. Some trees are close to the path, easy to touch and understand, while others stand a bit farther away, shrouded in the complexity of different backgrounds and experiences. Empathy is the bridge that allows you to reach each tree, to touch and understand it, regardless of the distance. This deep, intrinsic connection is foundational to personal relationships and fostering effective interactions in our increasingly global society. In this chapter, we explore the transformative power of empathy, beginning with the art of active listening. This skill allows us to hear the words others say and the emotions and intentions behind them.

ACTIVE LISTENING SKILLS FOR EMPATHETIC ENGAGEMENT

The Fundamentals of Active Listening

Active listening is a dynamic process that requires you to fully concentrate, understand, respond, and remember what is being said. This is not about merely hearing words but about engaging with and processing the emotional content of the conversation. It's a skill that forms the bedrock of empathy, allowing you to connect with others on a deeper level. When you listen actively, you give your full attention to the speaker, using verbal and nonverbal cues to show engagement and comprehension. This practice helps to understand the other person's perspective and validates their feelings, making them feel respected and heard.

In practice, active listening involves several vital behaviors. These include maintaining eye contact, nodding to indicate understanding, and using small verbal confirmations like "yes" or "I see." It also involves mirroring the speaker's emotions with your facial expressions, which can help convey empathy and understanding. Moreover, paraphrasing what the speaker has said and asking open-ended questions to clarify points ensures that you have grasped the content accurately, providing them with an opportunity to elaborate further. This level of engagement makes conversations more meaningful and effective, fostering stronger connections and deeper understanding.

Barriers to Effective Listening

Despite its importance, active listening is often hindered by several barriers. Common obstacles include external distractions like noise or interruptions and internal interruptions like wandering thoughts or preconceived notions about the speaker or the topic. These barriers can disrupt the listening process, leading to misunderstandings and a lack of connection.

To overcome these barriers, creating a conducive environment for conversation is crucial. This may mean choosing a quiet place or minimizing potential interruptions before engaging in meaningful discussions. Internally, it requires managing your thoughts and emotions, setting aside judgments, and focusing on the speaker's words and feelings. Awareness of biases and setting them aside can significantly enhance your listening ability, allowing for a more genuine and empathetic engagement.

Practicing Active Listening

Developing active listening skills requires deliberate practice and mindfulness. One effective exercise for enhancing your active listening is the "reflection technique," where you reflect the speaker's words in your own words. This practice shows you are listening and ensures you understand the message correctly. Daily mindfulness exercises can also improve your focus and attentiveness, making it easier to stay present in conversations.

Another practical exercise is to engage in conversations with the explicit goal of understanding rather than responding. This shifts your focus from formulating your subsequent response to genuinely listening and absorbing what the speaker is saying. Over time, these practices can significantly improve your listening skills, making your interactions more effective and empathetic.

Active Listening in Difficult Conversations

Active listening becomes crucial in emotionally charged or difficult conversations where misunderstandings can escalate tensions. In such scenarios, maintaining a calm demeanor and showing genuine interest in understanding the other person's point of view can help de-escalate the situation. Acknowledging the emotions involved and validating the speaker's feelings without necessarily agreeing with their viewpoint is important. This can build a bridge of trust and openness, even in challenging interactions.

Strategies like pausing before responding, rephrasing emotional statements into neutral language, and openly acknowledging the difficulty of the conversation can also help maintain active listening during challenging discussions. By staying engaged and attentive, you foster an environment where constructive dialogue can occur, paving the way for resolution and mutual understanding.

In cultivating the skill of active listening, you enhance your ability to connect with others and deepen your empathetic engagement, enriching your personal and professional relationships. As we continue to explore the nuances of empathy in the following sections, remember that active listening is just the beginning of understanding and connecting with the world around you.

READING AND RESPONDING TO NONVERBAL CUES

Understanding nonverbal communication's subtle yet profound language is like decoding a hidden layer of human interaction beyond words. Nonverbal cues, which include facial expressions, body posture, gestures, eye contact, and even the physical distance between individuals, often convey much more than spoken language can. These cues offer invaluable insights into a person's emotions, intentions, and attitudes. For instance, a person may verbally agree, but their crossed arms and lack of eye contact might suggest hesitancy or disagreement. Recognizing and accurately interpreting these signals enhances your ability to connect with others on a deeper, more empathetic level.

Facial expressions are the most immediate and expressive means of communicating emotions. A smile indicates warmth and welcome, while furrowed brows suggest worry or concentration. Gestures also play a critical role; a nod can affirm engagement, while a wave can signal greeting or farewell. Posture, too, tells its own story—leaning forward can show interest, while slumping may indicate tiredness or disinterest. Learning to read these signs effectively requires careful observation and understanding of the context in which these cues occur. It's about noticing the congruence between verbal and nonverbal communication and using both to better understand the communicator's valid message.

It's worth noting that this section applies to neurotypical people. For neurodivergent people, it's often very difficult or even impossible to read these cues, and the nonverbal cues they project may give others a false impression as well. With the growing number of people affected by neurodivergence, it's important for you to be aware of the exceptions.

Consider the environment and the interaction context to hone your skill in interpreting nonverbal cues. For example, crossed arms during a casual conversation could indicate that the person is cold, not necessarily closed off or defensive. Practice observing people in various settings like cafés, meetings, or public transportation, and try to infer their emotions and interactions based only on their nonverbal signals. Over time, this practice can sharpen your intuition and significantly improve your understanding of others beyond the spoken word.

Responding to nonverbal cues is equally important as recognizing them. Your reactions can either foster a more significant connection or create distance. For instance, if someone appears closed off with arms crossed and minimal eye contact, acknowledging their discomfort (without verbalizing it) by giving them physical space or adopting a more open posture can help ease the interaction. Similarly, mirroring the positive body language of others, such as smiling or nodding, can create a rapport and encourage more open communication. The key is to respond in ways that respect and acknowledge the feelings and comfort levels of others, thereby enhancing mutual understanding and empathy.

Cultural differences significantly influence the interpretation and use of nonverbal cues. What is considered respectful and attentive in one culture may be perceived as intrusive or aggressive in another. For example, in many Western cultures, maintaining direct eye contact is seen as a sign of attentiveness and honesty. In contrast, in some Asian cultures, prolonged eye contact may be considered rude or confrontational. Therefore, being aware of these cultural nuances is crucial when interacting with people from different backgrounds. Educating yourself about these differences, asking respectful questions when unsure, and observing the norms practiced by others can help navigate these cultural variances. This sensitivity prevents potential misunderstandings and shows respect for diverse expressions of communication, fostering a more inclusive and empathetic interaction environment.

As you continue to engage with and adapt to the vast spectrum of nonverbal communication, remember that each gesture, expression, and posture is a piece of a larger puzzle. With practice and sensitivity, you can become fluent in this nonverbal language, enabling you to connect with others more effectively and empathetically, regardless of the spoken language.

EMPATHY IN CONFLICT RESOLUTION

Empathy, often misunderstood merely as a feeling of compassion or sorrow for someone else's hardships becomes a transformative tool when applied to conflict resolution. It involves a deeper engagement where you understand and share another person's feelings, stepping into their shoes, regardless of your opinion. This form of connection can significantly change the dynamics of a conflict, turning confrontations into opportunities for collaboration and deeper understanding. When you approach a conflict with empathy, you prioritize understanding the other person's perspective over winning the argument, which can lead to more sustainable and satisfactory resolutions for all parties involved.

In practical terms, using empathy to resolve conflicts involves a few critical steps that begin with temporarily setting aside your viewpoint to fully engage with the other person's emotional experience. This doesn't mean you agree with them, but rather that you acknowledge their feelings as valid. For instance, in a workplace conflict where a team member feels overlooked for contributions, recognizing their feelings of undervaluation can open up a dialogue that addresses deeper issues in team recognition and communication practices. Here, expressing understanding might involve verbal affirmations acknowledging the person's feelings, such as, "It sounds like you feel unappreciated, and that's a tough feeling to deal with."

Once you have established a mutual understanding of each other's emotional states, you can explore solutions together. This could involve each party suggesting ways to address the concerns raised, ensuring both feel heard and valued. The key here is maintaining an empathetic stance throughout the discussion, often requiring active efforts to keep your defensive or combative instincts in check. This may involve regularly reminding yourself of the value of finding common ground or even taking brief pauses during the discussion to reflect on what has been said and to recenter your empathetic focus.

Maintaining empathy under the pressure of conflict is challenging, particularly in emotionally charged situations with high personal stakes. Techniques such as deep breathing or pausing the conversation to collect thoughts would be useful for keeping your composure. Another helpful strategy is to adopt a mindset of curiosity rather than defensiveness. This involves asking open-ended questions to better understand the other person's perspective and inviting them to elaborate on their feelings and needs. This approach not only defuses tension but also deepens mutual understanding, paving the way for a resolution that respects the needs and feelings of all parties.

Consider the story of Maya and John, co-workers involved in a project with overlapping responsibilities. Tensions arose when John accused Maya of overstepping her bounds, while Maya felt that John was not communicating effectively. Their manager intervened empathetically, letting each party express their feelings without interruption or judgment. After both had spoken, the manager helped them identify their primary concerns—more explicit boundaries and better communication channels. They could agree on a plan that addressed their mutual needs by focusing on these shared goals rather than personal grievances. This instance resolved the conflict and improved their working relationship by fostering deeper mutual understanding and respect.

This example underscores how empathy can transform potential conflicts into opportunities for growth and connection. By prioritizing understanding and validating feelings, you can navigate conflicts not as battles to be won but as chances to deepen relationships and build collaborative solutions. As you continue to harness the power of empathy in conflict resolution, remember that each conflict presents an opportunity to strengthen connections, build trust, and create a more cooperative community, whether at work, at home, or in broader social interactions.

BUILDING EMPATHY IN DIGITAL COMMUNICATIONS

In the vast expanse of digital communication, where emails replace verbal conversations and social media stands in for face-to-face interactions, conveying genuine empathy presents unique challenges. Unlike in-person interactions, digital platforms strip away much of the nonverbal cues, such as tone, facial expressions, and body language, which are essential in understanding emotions and intentions. This lack of sensory information can make digital communications feel impersonal and detached, often leading to misunderstandings or a perceived lack of empathy. Furthermore, the immediacy and permanence of digital communications mean that messages can be sent in a moment of emotion and cannot be taken back, sometimes exacerbating conflicts or hurt feelings.

The first step is consciously adopting empathetic language to navigate these challenges and enhance empathy in digital interactions. This involves more than choosing the right words; it's about crafting your message with the reader's emotions in mind. Start by personalizing your communication. Use the recipient's name, reference past interactions, and show genuine interest in their situation. For instance, instead of a generic "Hope you're well," you could say, "I hope your love for gardening brought you comfort this weekend." This shows you remember personal details, making digital communication feel more personal and connected.

Another critical aspect is re-reading your messages before sending them, considering how they might be interpreted. Look for phrases that could be perceived as harsh or judgmental and rephrase them to be more supportive and understanding. For example, replace a direct command like "Send me the report by tomorrow" with a more considerate request, "Could you please send me the report by tomorrow? I appreciate your help with this tight deadline." Such adjustments, while subtle, can significantly soften the tone and make the recipient feel respected and understood.

The tone of your digital communications is crucial in conveying empathy. Since recipients can't hear your voice or see your facial expressions, your choice of words and sentence structure are vital in setting the right tone. Avoid all caps, excessive punctuation, or terse replies, as these can be interpreted as shouting or irritation. Instead, use softer, more inclusive language and phrases that invite dialogue and show openness to discussion. Phrases like "I understand where you're coming from" or "Let's work together to solve this" can go a long way in making your digital communications feel more empathetic and cooperative.

Consider practicing role-playing exercises with a friend or colleague to improve your empathetic communication in digital formats. Set up scenarios where you exchange emails or messages in a controlled environment, then provide feedback to each other on the empathy demonstrated in those communications. This exercise can help you become more aware of your habitual language and tone and refine them to be more empathetic. Also, maintaining a personal log where you reflect on your daily digital interactions can help you become more conscious of how you use language and tone over time, enhancing your ability to communicate empathetically.

Digital communication, despite its challenges, also offers a unique opportunity to practice and spread empathy on a scale never before possible. Empathetically communicating contributes to a more understanding and compassionate digital world. As you continue to engage with others online, remember that behind every screen is a person, perhaps not so different from yourself, navigating their path through the world.

MAKE A DIFFERENCE WITH YOUR REVIEW
EMOTIONAL INTELLIGENCE UNLOCKED

"Knowing yourself is the beginning of all wisdom."

ARISTOTLE

People who help others without expecting anything in return live happier and longer lives. So, if we can do that together, I'm all in!

To make that happen, I have a question for you...

Would you help someone you've never met, even if you never got credit for it?

Who is this person, you ask? They are like you. Or, at least, like you used to be. They want to make a difference, they need help, but they're not sure where to start.

Our mission is to make *Emotional Intelligence Unlocked* accessible to everyone. Everything we do comes from that mission. And the only way to accomplish it is by reaching... well... everyone. This is where you come in. Most people do, in fact, judge a book by its cover (and its reviews). So here's my ask on behalf of all the people you've never met who are trying to improve their lives:

Please help that person get ahead in life by leaving this book a review.

Your gift costs no money and takes less than sixty seconds, but it can change a person's life forever. Your review could help...

...one more person transform their life

...one more dream come true

To get that "feel-good" feeling and help this person for real, all you have to do is... and it takes less than sixty seconds... leave a review.

Simply scan the QR code below to leave your review:

If you feel good about helping a faceless person trying to improve their life, you are my kind of person. Welcome to the club. You're one of us.

I'm that much more excited to help you live your best life as quickly and meaningfully as possible. You'll love the lessons and strategies I'm about to share in the coming chapters.

Thank you from the bottom of my heart. Now, back to our regularly scheduled programming.

Your biggest fan,

Liam Grant

CHAPTER 6
COMMUNICATION MASTERY WITH EQ

In the tapestry of human interaction, each communication thread weaves a pattern that can bind us closer to others or fray the edges of our relationships. Mastering the art of communication is akin to a skilled weaver who knows how to pull each thread to create a harmonious design. This chapter delves into the nuanced skills of emotional articulation—a process by which you learn to express your emotions precisely and effectively, enhancing your connections and enriching your interactions.

THE ART OF EMOTIONAL ARTICULATION

Expressing Emotions Clearly and Effectively

The cornerstone of effective communication lies in your ability to articulate your emotions with clarity and precision. This isn't just about letting others know how you feel; it's about sharing your inner world in an understandable and relatable way. Using "I" statements is a powerful tool in this process. These statements allow you to express your feelings without casting blame or creating defensiveness. For example, saying, "I feel overwhelmed when meetings run late without advance notice," directly communicates your emotions and the situation affecting them without implying fault. This method clarifies your emotional state and opens the door for more constructive and empathetic dialogue.

The language you choose is pivotal in how your message is received. Specificity in language prevents ambiguity, helping the listener understand your emotional experience more accurately. Instead of saying, "I'm upset," which is vague and open to interpretation, specifying, "I'm disheartened by how this situation was handled," provides a clear insight into your emotional reaction. This specificity not only aids in mutual understanding but also enhances the emotional depth of your interactions, fostering stronger relational ties.

Balancing Emotional Expression

While expressing your emotions is essential, maintaining a balance in how these emotions are conveyed is equally critical. This balance involves respecting and valuing the feelings and perspectives of the listener while sharing your own. It's about achieving a harmony in which your emotions are not diluted by fear of overshadowing others' feelings, nor are they expressed too forcefully, which could lead to discomfort or misunderstanding.

This equilibrium can be achieved through empathetic engagement —where you remain attuned to the listener's reactions as you share your emotions. This does not mean you take responsibility for their emotional responses, but rather that you are considerate and mindful of how your words might impact them. For instance, if you observe signs of discomfort or defensiveness, modulating your tone or pausing to invite feedback may be beneficial, ensuring the communication remains a dialogue rather than a monologue.

Articulation Exercises: Enhancing Emotional Expression

Engaging in specific exercises can be incredibly beneficial to refine your emotional articulation skills. Reflective writing is an exercise where you regularly jot down your feelings about daily events. This practice helps clarify and organize your thoughts and discover the most accurate words to describe your emotions. Try to detail what happened, how you felt, and why you think you felt that way, linking your feelings to your thoughts and experiences.

Role-playing scenarios offer another dynamic way to practice emotional articulation. By acting out conversations with a friend or a therapist, you can explore various ways of expressing the same emotion, seeing firsthand the impact of different word choices and delivery styles. These rehearsals can boost your confidence and skill in real-life situations, making you more adept at expressing your emotions clearly and effectively.

Overcoming Fear of Emotional Expression

Many individuals fear expressing their emotions, often worrying about potential conflict, rejection, or being perceived as weak. Overcoming this fear is crucial for authentic and meaningful communication. One effective strategy is gradual exposure, where you start by expressing minor emotions in safe environments and gradually work up to more significant feelings or more challenging settings. This process reduces anxiety around emotional expression and builds confidence.

Additionally, cognitive restructuring can help reshape the beliefs that underlie the fear of emotional expression. By challenging thoughts like "If I express sadness, I'll be seen as weak" and replacing them with more balanced beliefs, such as "Expressing sadness is a natural and healthy way to communicate my feelings," you can change your emotional landscape and become more open in your communications.

Engaging in these practices enhances your ability to articulate emotions and deepens your emotional intelligence, allowing for more meaningful and satisfying interactions in both personal and professional contexts. As you continue to develop these skills, remember that each step forward enriches your communication abilities, making every conversation a bridge to greater understanding and connection.

ASSERTIVE COMMUNICATION: SPEAKING YOUR TRUTH WITHOUT HARM

Assertive communication is a style that allows you to express your thoughts, feelings, and needs in a straightforward and respectful way. It stands distinct from passive communication, where one might suppress one's desires to avoid conflict, and aggressive communication, where the focus is on winning the argument, often at the expense of others' feelings. Assertive communication is about balance—it respects both your rights and those of others, fostering a dialogue where everyone feels valued and heard.

Understanding and implementing assertive communication can significantly enhance your relationships. It creates a platform where open and honest dialogue is encouraged and expected. This transparency helps build trust and prevent resentments, which often arise from unspoken frustrations or misunderstood intentions. When you communicate assertively, you directly address issues as they arise, preventing minor misunderstandings from escalating into more significant conflicts. Moreover, it empowers both parties by giving each a voice, ensuring that decisions affecting the relationship consider the needs and feelings of all involved.

When aiming to communicate assertively, your choice of words and how you deliver them play a pivotal role. Clear, concise language helps prevent ambiguity in your messages, making your intentions and feelings understandable. Begin statements with "I feel" or "I believe," indicating that you are speaking from your perspective without presumptions about the other person's feelings or intentions. This approach keeps the focus on your experience and lessens the likelihood of the listener feeling accused or defensive.

Your body language also significantly impacts how your message is received. Maintaining an open posture, with uncrossed arms and steady, non-confrontational eye contact, can reinforce the sincerity and respect you aim to communicate. These nonverbal cues can enhance the clarity and effectiveness of your spoken words, reinforcing your assertive message.

Practicing assertiveness can initially feel daunting, especially if you are accustomed to a more passive or aggressive communication style. Role-playing exercises are an excellent way to build your confidence in this area. These scenarios provide a safe space to experiment with and refine your assertiveness skills. For example, you might role-play a situation where you must refuse a friend's unreasonable request. Practicing how to say "no" firmly but kindly can prepare you for real-life situations where you might need to set boundaries.

Another scenario is asking for a raise at work. This situation typically requires a careful balance of assertiveness, where you must clearly state your achievements and request a salary that reflects your value without coming across as demanding. Role-playing this conversation with a mentor or peer can help you find the right words and tone to use, making you feel more prepared and confident when discussing it with your employer.

Regular practice of these scenarios will gradually enhance your comfort and skill in assertive communication, making it easier to navigate various interpersonal interactions with grace and effectiveness. As you apply these principles, you'll likely notice a positive relationship shift characterized by more open dialogue, increased mutual respect, and fewer misunderstandings. This shift enhances your personal and professional relationships. It contributes to greater self-esteem as you become more adept at expressing your needs and boundaries clearly and respectfully.

THE POWER OF VULNERABILITY IN DEEPENING CONNECTIONS

Vulnerability often carries a heavy cloak of myths and misconceptions, the most common being that it signifies weakness or emotional fragility. In reality, vulnerability is the willingness to express one's true self, encompassing feelings, desires, fears, and uncertainties, without succumbing to the societal masks that often dictate superficial interactions. It's about being open and authentic about your thoughts and emotions, which requires immense courage and strength. This honesty invites a deeper level of trust and facilitates a genuine connection that can significantly enhance the quality of relationships. When you share your vulnerabilities, you signal to others that they are in a safe space to unveil their true selves, fostering a mutual exchange of authenticity.

Understanding Vulnerability

Redefining what it means is essential to truly harness the strength of vulnerability. Vulnerability does not mean oversharing or exposing oneself to harm but rather selectively opening up to foster trust and understanding. It involves sharing personal insights or emotions that can feel risky to disclose but do so in a way that deepens connections. It's important to distinguish this from weakness, which often implies a lack of strength or capability. Vulnerability, in contrast, is a deliberate choice to build emotional depth, strengthening interpersonal dynamics. By debunking the myth that vulnerability is a flaw, you can start to see it as a powerful tool in your emotional intelligence arsenal that can transform how you interact with others.

Vulnerability as a Strength

Embracing vulnerability can paradoxically lead to more robust, more resilient relationships. Opening up to someone and showing your true self, including your imperfections and doubts, creates a space for authenticity. This authenticity invites others to reciprocate, paving the way for deeper emotional connections. In a professional setting, a leader's vulnerability can humanize them, bridging the gap between authority and approachability. This can enhance loyalty and morale among team members who feel they are seen and understood beyond their professional roles. In personal relationships, vulnerability fosters intimacy and trust, creating a solid foundation to withstand the inevitable challenges that arise within close connections.

Exercises for Embracing Vulnerability

Becoming comfortable and vulnerable is a gradual process, which can be nurtured through specific exercises designed to ease you into this practice. One practical approach is using vulnerability circles, a space where a small group of people agree to share personal stories or feelings without judgment. These circles can be set up among friends, family, or coworkers, with clear ground rules to ensure confidentiality and respect. Another exercise is the "three truths" activity, where you share three personal truths and one falsehood with a partner, who then guesses which is untrue. This game-like scenario provides a lighter, engaging way to practice vulnerability.

Journaling can also serve as a private, reflective practice for exploring vulnerabilities. Writing down your fears, aspirations, and uncertainties helps clarify your thoughts and emotions, making it easier to share them with others when you're ready. Over time, these exercises can help desensitize the discomfort associated with vulnerability, making it easier to open yourself up to the people who matter most in your life.

Setting Boundaries When Being Vulnerable

While vulnerability can enhance connections, setting boundaries to protect your emotional well-being is crucial. Not all environments or individuals are conducive to safe emotional exposure. It's important to assess the trustworthiness and empathy levels of those with whom you choose to be vulnerable. Setting boundaries may mean deciding what, how much, and to whom you choose to reveal personal thoughts or feelings. It also involves recognizing when to step back if the emotional exchange becomes one-sided or your openness is not met with respect or care.

A practical way to set these boundaries is to start small. Share something moderately personal and gauge the reaction. If the response is empathetic and supportive, gradually opening up more might be safe. However, if the reaction is dismissive or judgmental, it's a clear indicator to reinforce your boundaries. This selective approach ensures that your practice of vulnerability is intentional and protected, allowing you to open up without compromising your emotional safety.

As you continue to navigate the complexities of emotional interactions, remember that vulnerability is not just about revealing yourself; it's about enriching your connections through the courageous act of authenticity. This dynamic interplay of openness and boundary-setting deepens your relationships and fosters a profound understanding of yourself and those around you.

TRANSFORMATIVE CONVERSATIONS: EQ TECHNIQUES THAT FACILITATE CHANGE

Transformative conversations are rare dialogues that leave an indelible mark on our relationships and personal growth. They are not just exchanges of information but interactions that foster real change and deepen understanding. At the heart of such conversations are key elements like empathy, active listening, and an openness to change, each pivotal in transforming dialogue into a powerful tool for personal and relational evolution.

Empathy in transformative conversations acts as a bridge, connecting disparate viewpoints through the shared experience of emotions. It allows you to step into another's shoes, see the world through their eyes, and respond to their feelings with understanding and care. This empathetic engagement is complemented by active listening, which involves fully concentrating on what is being said rather than passively hearing the words. It means listening with all senses, responding with thoughtful insights, and acknowledging the speaker's feelings and perspectives. Lastly, openness to change is essential; it involves embracing the possibility that the conversation could lead to personal or mutual change. This openness does not mean compromising your values but requires a willingness to evolve your understanding and behavior in light of new insights.

Facilitating change through dialogue requires a nuanced approach in which emotionally intelligent conversations become catalysts for transformation. Such dialogues encourage exploration and questioning of old patterns, inviting new ways of thinking that can lead to significant shifts in attitude and behavior. For instance, a conversation about workplace dynamics can lead to a deeper understanding of interpersonal relationships and prompt changes in communication strategies or conflict resolution methods. The key to facilitating such change is creating a safe environment where all parties feel valued and heard, making navigation through uncomfortable or challenging topics easier.

Navigating resistance or defensiveness is often the most challenging aspect of conversations about change. Resistance can surface as a natural reaction to perceived threats to one's self-concept or ideas. Fostering an atmosphere of mutual respect and assurance is essential to manage this. Techniques such as affirming the other person's feelings, reframing the conversation from a different perspective, or taking breaks when the emotional intensity escalates can be effective. Additionally, focusing on the benefits of change rather than the drawbacks can help reduce resistance, illustrating not what will be lost but what will be gained from adapting to new ways of thinking or behaving.

Consider a case where two business partners frequently clash over strategic decisions. A transformative conversation might involve each partner expressing their underlying fears and motivations, facilitated by a mediator skilled in empathetic listening and reframing issues in a non-confrontational manner. Through such a dialogue, the partners may discover that their conflicts stem not from differing business visions but incompatible communication styles. Recognizing this difference can shift the nature of their interactions, leading to more productive discussions and a strengthened partnership.

As you integrate these techniques into your conversations, remember that the goal is not to win an argument but to foster understanding and growth. Each dialogue offers a unique opportunity to solve problems, enrich relationships, and expand personal horizons. By approaching conversations with empathy, listening actively, and being open to change, you set the stage for meaningful transformations that can profoundly impact your personal and professional life.

To wrap up this chapter, we've explored how mastering emotional articulation, assertiveness, and vulnerability can significantly enhance your communication skills. These capabilities are crucial for everyday interactions and for fostering deeper and more meaningful connections. As we move forward, we will explore how these enhanced communication skills can be effectively applied to build and maintain personal relationships, creating a foundation for lasting bonds and mutual growth.

CHAPTER 7
BUILDING AND MAINTAINING PERSONAL RELATIONSHIPS

In the garden of life, personal relationships are the delicate blooms that require nurturing, care, and a keen understanding of the emotional soil from which they grow. Just as a gardener learns to understand the unique needs of each plant, mastering the art of maintaining personal relationships—especially romantic ones—relies on a deep understanding of emotional intelligence. This chapter unwraps the layers of EQ strategies that sustain and enrich romantic partnerships, ensuring they flourish through seasons of sunshine and rain.

EQ STRATEGIES FOR ROMANTIC PARTNERSHIPS

Understanding Your Partner's Emotional Needs

Every romantic relationship is a unique interplay of emotions, where understanding and responding to your partner's emotional needs becomes the cornerstone of a lasting bond. At its heart, EQ involves profoundly recognizing and reacting to these needs, which often requires peeling back layers of spoken and unspoken communication. Active listening paired with empathetic responsiveness is crucial to truly grasp your partner's feelings and needs. It's about hearing unspoken words and recognizing the emotions behind the façade of day-to-day interactions. This may mean noticing a sigh that belies stress or a smile that doesn't quite reach the eyes and gently probing to uncover the underlying feelings. Regular, open conversations about each other's emotional states foster a deeper understanding and show a committed effort to meet halfway, nurturing the relationship's growth.

Communication in Romance

Effective communication in romantic relationships extends beyond mere words; it's an emotional dialogue that builds intimacy and understanding. Incorporating EQ into your communication involves being attuned to your own emotions and those of your partner and expressing these emotions constructively. Techniques like "emotional mirroring"—reflecting your partner's emotions through verbal and nonverbal cues—can enhance emotional synchrony. For instance, acknowledging your partner's excitement about a new project with genuine interest and enthusiasm can amplify their joy. Moreover, integrating phrases emphasizing emotional understanding, such as "I can see how important this is to you," validates their feelings and deepens their emotional connection. Regularly engaging in emotionally intelligent dialogues can transform simple exchanges into profound interactions, laying a solid foundation for enduring intimacy.

Conflict Resolution with EQ

Conflicts can strengthen rather than strain a relationship when navigated with emotional intelligence. The key lies in addressing disputes, focusing on empathy and collaborative problem-solving rather than contention. Begin by expressing your feelings and concerns using "I" statements, which reduce the likelihood of the other person feeling attacked and becoming defensive. For example, saying, "I feel hurt when decisions are made without my input," clearly states your feelings without blaming others. Follow this by actively seeking your partner's perspective and striving for a mutual understanding. This approach minimizes emotional damage and turns conflicts into opportunities for learning and growth within the relationship. It's about finding solutions that respect both partners' feelings and needs, fortifying the relationship against future discord.

Maintaining Connection Over Time

Sustaining emotional connection over time, particularly through challenging periods, demands continuous nurturing of the relationship's emotional roots. This involves consistently investing time and effort into understanding and adapting to evolving emotional needs. Establish regular check-ins with your partner to discuss day-to-day life and deeper emotional currents. These moments of connection are vital for reaffirming commitment and re-aligning with each other's emotional landscapes. Additionally, engaging in shared activities that foster joy and companionship can reinforce the emotional bond. Whether it's a hobby, a class, or regular date nights, these activities provide opportunities to create joyful memories and strengthen the emotional glue that holds the relationship together.

In weaving these EQ strategies into the fabric of your romantic relationship, you cultivate a partnership characterized by deep understanding, effective communication, and resilient love. Each strategy is a thread in the tapestry of your shared life, colored by emotions and patterns that you choose together. By continuously nurturing these emotional connections, you ensure that the relationship survives and thrives, enriched by the mutual effort and understanding that define true emotional intelligence.

NAVIGATING FAMILY DYNAMICS WITH EMOTIONAL INTELLIGENCE

Each member plays a distinct role in the intricate web of family life, influenced by their personality, life experiences, and how they interpret their place within the family hierarchy. Understanding these roles through the lens of emotional intelligence can significantly enhance family dynamics, promoting a more harmonious home environment. Recognizing and respecting the diverse emotional landscapes each family member navigates helps foster acceptance and reduce conflicts. For instance, considering why a typically reserved sibling may prefer quieter engagements can help plan family activities that everyone enjoys. Similarly, acknowledging a parent's concerns about security and stability can lead to more productive conversations about riskier activities or financial decisions. This nuanced understanding of family roles, informed by EQ, does not just accommodate but celebrates individual differences, ensuring each member feels valued and understood.

Addressing family conflicts with EQ involves a proactive approach that prioritizes emotional understanding and effective resolution strategies. Conflicts often arise from misunderstood intentions or unmet emotional needs rather than the surface issues. By focusing first on understanding the emotional undercurrents—such as fear, frustration, or need for recognition—you can address the root cause of the conflict more effectively. Active listening plays a crucial role here; it involves giving undivided attention to the family members, expressing their concerns, reflecting on their feelings, and validating their experiences without immediate judgment or solutions. This approach clarifies misunderstandings and strengthens emotional bonds, as family members feel genuinely heard and understood. Moreover, conflict resolution strategies emphasizing collaborative problem-solving can transform conflicts from divisive to developmental experiences. For example, using "we" statements like "We can work together to find a solution" instead of "You need to fix this" fosters a team mentality that encourages cooperative behavior and collective resolution.

Encouraging and supporting emotional growth within the family is another pivotal aspect of using EQ. This involves creating a supportive environment where expressing emotions and personal challenges is safe and welcomed. Encourage regular family discussions that involve sharing feelings, challenges, and achievements. These discussions can be structured through family meetings where members share one high and one low of their week, fostering a routine normalizing open emotional expression. Additionally, modeling emotional intelligence as a parent or guardian—such as expressing your emotions healthily, showing empathy for others' feelings, and admitting when you're wrong—is a powerful example for children and teenagers. By embedding emotional learning in everyday interactions, you help teach EQ naturally to family members, equipping them with the emotional skills necessary to navigate personal and professional relationships effectively.

Creating an emotionally intelligent family environment does not mean enforcing a constant state of peace or suppressing conflicts; instead, it means fostering an atmosphere where understanding and managing emotions are prioritized. This can be facilitated by integrating practices like mindfulness exercises that enhance emotional awareness or setting up an "emotion corner" in the home where family members can calm down and reflect when feeling overwhelmed. Additionally, celebrating emotional victories—such as effectively handling a challenging situation or successfully employing a new communication technique—reinforces the importance of EQ in everyday life. These practices improve individual emotional skills and enhance the family's collective emotional health, making it a stronger, more understanding unit.

Navigating family dynamics with emotional intelligence is about cultivating a garden where every member, regardless of their unique emotional flora, can thrive. By applying EQ to understand and respect individual emotional needs, resolve conflicts constructively, foster emotional growth, and create a supportive family environment, you lay the groundwork for a family life that is not only functional but also deeply fulfilling. This approach solves immediate family issues and sows the seeds for lifelong emotional intelligence that will continue to benefit family members in all areas of their lives.

DEEPENING FRIENDSHIPS WITH EMOTIONAL AWARENESS

The fabric of deep and enduring friendships is often woven with threads of emotional intelligence. EQ is a critical tool in these relationships, enhancing understanding and empathy and fostering connections that thrive on mutual respect and emotional support. Recognizing and practicing EQ in friendships can transform casual acquaintances into cherished confidants and turn fleeting interactions into lasting bonds.

At the core of using EQ in friendships is the ability to discern and respond to the emotional cues of your friends. This sensitivity allows you to navigate through the layers of communication, understanding what is being said and what is left unspoken. For instance, when a friend talks about their busy day with a smile, but their eyes reflect fatigue, EQ prompts you to respond to their underlying need —perhaps offering a listening ear or a helping hand—rather than simply acknowledging their words. This depth of interaction, where emotional cues guide responses, fosters a more prosperous, supportive friendship.

Empathetic listening is a cornerstone of such emotionally intelligent friendships. It involves more than hearing words; it's about engaging fully with the friend's experiences and emotions. To enhance empathetic listening among friends, focus on being fully present. This may mean setting aside your phone during conversations or consciously steering clear of crafting responses in your mind while your friend is still speaking. Instead, let their words guide your reactions, and use reflective listening techniques. For example, if a friend expresses frustration about a work issue, respond with, "It sounds like you're overwhelmed with this project," rather than immediately offering solutions. Such responses validate their feelings and show you are genuinely engaged with their experiences.

Another area where EQ can be invaluable is supporting friends through personal challenges or crises. When friends face difficulties, how you respond can deepen the relationship or create distance. Start by acknowledging their distress and asking how you can help, which shows that you are there for them in a meaningful way. It's important to offer support that aligns with their needs, from being a sounding board to taking on practical tasks or simply providing company. Remember, sometimes the most potent form of support is being present and attentive without pushing for action or dismissing their feelings. These moments, where you stand with them in their challenges, solidify trust and deepen the emotional connection.

Building a circle of emotionally intelligent friends creates a supportive network that fosters personal growth and emotional well-being. Start by embodying the qualities of emotional intelligence yourself, such as empathy, authenticity, and emotional awareness, which naturally attracts like-minded individuals. Encourage open discussions about emotions and vulnerabilities in your social circles, which can set a precedent for honesty and emotional depth in interactions. Organize group activities that promote emotional sharing and reflection, such as book clubs focused on personal development or group outings that include time for sharing personal stories. Over time, these practices cultivate a group dynamic that values and practices emotional intelligence, creating a community where members support and uplift each other.

Nurturing these emotionally intelligent friendships enriches your social interactions and creates a supportive network that enhances your collective emotional resilience. These friendships, rooted in mutual understanding and emotional support, often provide the most comfort and joy. They are the relationships that endure through life's ups and downs, offering solace and celebration at every turn. By prioritizing emotional awareness in your friendships, you invest in building a community that understands and genuinely supports the emotional well-being of all its members.

HANDLING BREAKUPS AND LOSS THROUGH EQ

Emotional resilience in the context of personal loss, whether from a breakup or the death of a loved one, requires a robust foundation in emotional intelligence. That means cultivating the ability to navigate through intense emotions with understanding and self-compassion. Building this kind of resilience begins with acknowledging and accepting your feelings, whatever they may be—sadness, anger, confusion, or even relief. Recognizing these feelings as natural responses to loss is crucial; suppressing them only strengthens those feelings. Instead, allow yourself the space to experience them fully. This may involve setting aside private times for reflection or using expressive writing to articulate your feelings. Both strategies serve as outlets for emotional release and are essential to building resilience. Moreover, integrating mindfulness practices can significantly aid this process. Techniques such as mindful breathing or guided meditation create moments of calm and presence, helping to manage and mitigate overwhelming feelings and providing a grounding effect during emotional turbulence.

Navigating the aftermath of a breakup or loss also requires effective strategies for managing complex emotions. One practical approach is to structure your days to include activities that foster a sense of normalcy and continuity. While it's important to acknowledge and respect your grief, creating a balance with structured, routine activities can provide necessary breaks from intense emotions. Physical activities, such as walking or yoga, keep you grounded in your body and promote the release of endorphins, which can improve mood and reduce stress. Additionally, staying connected with supportive friends or family can provide essential emotional support. Sometimes, simply having someone listen to your experiences and emotions without judgment can provide immense relief and aid in healing. It's also beneficial to gradually expose yourself to new experiences and social settings. While this may feel daunting, engaging with life outside of your grief can help foster resilience and emotional recovery, reminding you that life's richness is multifaceted and continues beyond loss.

Emotional growth from the experience of loss is a profound journey of self-discovery. This process often involves reevaluating personal values, beliefs, and the meaning you assign to experiences. Emotional intelligence plays a pivotal role here, allowing you to reflect on how the experience has shaped you. Ask yourself, "What has this loss taught me about my needs and desires?" or "How has this experience shaped my understanding of relationships?" Reflecting on these questions can transform pain into insightful learning, fostering personal growth. This introspection can lead to a deeper understanding of yourself and your emotional needs, potentially guiding you toward future relationships more aligned with your true self. Furthermore, embracing a growth mindset and openness to change can encourage you to apply these insights practically, enhancing your overall emotional intelligence and readiness for new relationships.

Supporting others through their experiences of loss is another significant aspect of emotional intelligence. It involves a delicate balance of being present, listening actively, and offering support without imposing your interpretations of their feelings. Start by simply being there for them, offering a supportive presence that reassures them they are not alone. Listening is more about hearing their feelings and stories without rushing to offer advice. When you offer support, ensure it is attuned to their needs—ask them how you can help instead of assuming you know what's best for them. Support may sometimes mean sitting in silence together, providing a comforting presence. If you're unsure what to say, expressing genuine statements like, "I'm here for you" or "I'm just a call away if you need to talk" can be profoundly comforting. Remember, the goal is not to fix their pain but to walk them through it, offering empathy and understanding, which can be incredibly healing.

As we close this chapter, we reflect on the profoundly transformative potential of emotional intelligence in navigating the deeply personal terrains of breakups and loss. By understanding and managing our emotions, supporting others, and using our experiences for personal growth, we recover and emerge more resilient and emotionally aware. These skills are important for recovery; they enhance our overall capacity for empathy and connection, enriching our lives and those of others around us. As we transition into the next chapter, we will explore how emotional intelligence influences and enhances workplace dynamics, and we will offer professional growth and success strategies.

CHAPTER 8
EMOTIONAL INTELLIGENCE IN THE WORKPLACE

Imagine entering a workplace where each interaction, decision, and leadership directive is infused with empathy, understanding, and genuine concern for emotional well-being. This isn't a far-off utopia but a tangible reality that can be achieved through the strategic application of emotional intelligence. In today's fast-paced and often impersonal business environment, EQ emerges as a beneficial attribute and a fundamental necessity for fostering a thriving workplace culture. This chapter delves into the transformative role of emotional intelligence in leadership—a paradigm where leading with EQ is not merely an option but an essential strategy for success.

LEADING WITH EMOTIONAL INTELLIGENCE: A NEW PARADIGM

The EQ Leader: What It Means to Lead with Emotional Intelligence and the Advantages It Brings

Leadership, at its core, is about influencing others, and what better way to influence than through the power of emotional intelligence? An EQ leader embodies the ability to manage personal emotions as well as understand and influence the feelings of others. This leadership style fosters an environment of trust and respect where employees feel valued and understood. The advantages of leading with EQ are manifold. Firstly, EQ leaders tend to have better relationships with their team members, which can lead to increased productivity and morale. Secondly, these leaders are typically more adaptable to change, a crucial attribute in today's ever-evolving business landscape. Their ability to sense and respond to shifts in team dynamics and market conditions allows for more agile and effective decision-making.

Developing EQ Leadership Skills: Strategies for Developing and Enhancing EQ Skills Essential for Leadership

Developing your EQ leadership skills is a journey of personal and professional growth. Key strategies include practicing self-awareness and reflection, which involve regular check-ins with oneself to understand personal emotional responses and triggers. Journaling can be a particularly effective tool, providing a private space to explore and understand your emotional reactions. Another important strategy is active listening, in which the listener entirely focuses on the speaker, understands their message, and responds thoughtfully. This skill improves communication and builds deeper relationships with team members, making them feel heard and respected. Additionally, empathy exercises, such as role-reversal scenarios where leaders put themselves in their employees' shoes, can deepen leaders' understanding of their teams' challenges, enhancing their ability to respond with compassion and support.

Case Studies of EQ in Leadership: Real-World Examples of Successful Leaders Who Exemplify Emotional Intelligence

Consider the case of a tech startup CEO who prioritized open emotional communication within her team. By regularly sharing her challenges and vulnerabilities in team meetings, she created a safe space for her employees to do the same. This practice reduced stress and anxiety among team members. It fostered a strong sense of community and loyalty within the team, leading to a 40 percent increase in productivity and a significant drop in employee turnover. Another example is a school principal who used empathy-driven leadership to transform a struggling school. By actively listening to the concerns of both teachers and students, he implemented new programs that addressed these concerns, such as peer mentoring and mental health days, leading to improved academic performance and a happier, more engaged school environment.

Creating an EQ-Focused Culture: How Leaders Can Foster an Organizational Culture That Values and Practices Emotional Intelligence

Creating an EQ-focused culture starts at the top. Leaders who openly demonstrate emotional intelligence set a powerful example for their teams, encouraging similar behaviors in their organizations. Regular training sessions on emotional intelligence can equip employees with the tools and knowledge they need to enhance their EQ skills. These include workshops on empathy, active listening, and emotional regulation, all crucial for a supportive and productive workplace. Additionally, incorporating EQ into the company's core values and performance evaluations can reinforce its importance, making it a fundamental aspect of the organizational culture. Recognizing and rewarding high-EQ behaviors, such as effective conflict resolution or exceptional team collaboration, also helps cement the importance of emotional intelligence in driving organizational success.

In this landscape of EQ-driven leadership and culture, the workplace transforms into a dynamic environment where emotional intelligence guides interactions and decisions, leading to a more harmonious, productive, and ultimately successful organization.

EQ IN TEAM DYNAMICS: FOSTERING HARMONY AND PRODUCTIVITY

In any team, the collective emotional state can often be as varied as it is volatile, influenced by individual team members' personalities, external pressures, and the ever-changing dynamics of the workplace. To effectively read and understand a team's emotional climate, you start by paying close attention to nonverbal cues, such as body language and facial expressions, which can provide significant insights into the team's overall mood and individual feelings. Maintaining open lines of communication where team members feel safe expressing their emotions is crucial. This can be facilitated through regular team meetings focused on emotional check-ins, where members are encouraged to share their feelings and concerns openly. By creating an environment that values emotional openness, you gain a clearer understanding of the team's emotional state and foster a culture that prioritizes emotional well-being.

To enhance communication and collaboration through EQ, it's essential to tailor your communication style to fit the team's emotional needs. This involves actively listening to each member's input and responding in a way that acknowledges and validates their emotions, promoting a sense of inclusivity and respect. Implementing collaborative tools and practices, such as shared goal-setting sessions during which team members can express their visions and reservations, helps ensure everyone feels their voice is heard and valued. These practices improve communication and deepen trust among team members, making collaboration more effective and efficient.

Conflict is inevitable in any team, but the manner of resolution can either strengthen or weaken the collective dynamic. Applying principles of emotional intelligence to resolve team conflicts involves identifying the emotional undercurrents that may be driving the conflict. This could be a sense of unfairness, frustration, or miscommunication. Addressing these emotional aspects directly, rather than focusing solely on the practical issues, can lead to more enduring resolutions. Techniques such as mediation sessions, where conflicting parties are encouraged to express their emotions and viewpoints openly, facilitated by a neutral party, can be particularly effective. These sessions aim not only to resolve the conflict but also to understand its emotional triggers, which can prevent future disputes.

Building a stronger, more cohesive team using EQ involves a continuous commitment to fostering an emotionally intelligent environment. This includes regular training and workshops on emotional intelligence skills, such as empathy, emotional regulation, and interpersonal communication. Investing in these skills builds a team that is not only more productive but also more resilient to the stresses of the workplace. Team-building activities that focus on emotional connection—such as retreats or collaborative projects that allow members to explore and express their emotions—can further strengthen this bond. These activities help transform a group of individuals into a unified team characterized by a shared emotional understanding and a strong, supportive work culture.

In essence, enhancing team dynamics through emotional intelligence is not a one-time fix; it means integrating EQ into the team's day-to-day interactions and operations. This integration transforms the workplace into a space where emotional awareness and mutual respect drive innovation and productivity, creating a team that is effective in achieving its goals and a joy to be part of.

MANAGING UPWARD: EQ STRATEGIES FOR DEALING WITH SUPERVISORS

Navigating the nuances of your relationship with your supervisor requires more than just understanding the tasks at hand; it demands a keen grasp of emotional intelligence. Perceiving and interpreting the emotional undertones of your interactions with those above you in the workplace hierarchy can significantly impact your professional development and daily work satisfaction. First, it's vital to gauge the level of emotional intelligence your supervisor exhibits. This understanding can guide how you communicate and collaborate with them. Observing how they handle stress, respond to feedback, and communicate in meetings can provide insights into their EQ capabilities. For instance, a supervisor who listens attentively to concerns and addresses them constructively is likely to have high emotional intelligence. In contrast, one who often reacts defensively or dismissively might need further EQ development.

Once you understand your supervisor's EQ better, tailoring your communication to align with their emotional strengths and weaknesses becomes crucial. If your supervisor values directness, ensure your communications are clear and to the point without forgoing polite formalities that convey respect. On the other hand, if they appreciate more detailed discussions, provide comprehensive updates that anticipate potential questions they may have. This strategy facilitates smoother interactions and builds a rapport based on mutual understanding and respect. Additionally, regular one-on-one meetings can be a strategic way to strengthen this communication channel, providing space for more personalized interaction and the opportunity to build a professional relationship grounded in emotional intelligence.

Approaching difficult conversations with your supervisor is one of the most challenging aspects of managing upward, yet it is essential for your career growth and workplace harmony. Preparation is vital; before such a meeting, take the time to clearly define the purpose of the conversation and anticipate possible reactions. During the discussion, employ EQ by actively listening, maintaining a calm demeanor, and expressing your points clearly and respectfully. Use "I" statements to express how specific situations affect your work or feelings, avoiding accusations or generalizations that could put your supervisor on the defensive. For example, instead of saying, "You never give me clear instructions," try, "I find it challenging to meet expectations when instructions aren't clear. Could we explore a way to improve clarity moving forward?" This approach keeps the conversation constructive and demonstrates your commitment to resolving the issue collaboratively.

Building and maintaining a positive relationship with your supervisor through emotional intelligence can transform your work environment and propel your professional growth. This involves more than just managing direct interactions; it extends to understanding and respecting their leadership style and professional pressures. Demonstrating reliability in your work, showing initiative, and expressing appreciation for their guidance can reinforce a positive dynamic. Additionally, being empathetic toward the challenges in their role can foster deeper professional respect and open the door for more supportive interactions. By consistently applying these EQ strategies, you create a working relationship that is functional and enriching, marked by mutual respect and collaborative success.

NAVIGATING OFFICE POLITICS WITH GRACE AND WISDOM

Office politics, a seemingly inevitable part of working within any organization, often conjures images of backdoor dealings and competitive maneuvering. However, when approached with high emotional intelligence, navigating this complex landscape can become less about survival and more about strategic relationship-building. Understanding the emotional undercurrents that drive office politics can provide valuable insights into the motivations and behaviors of your colleagues. High EQ enables you to decode these dynamics, allowing you to anticipate potential conflicts and align with others' emotional needs and desires, which can be important for advancing projects and gaining support.

Staying above the fray of office politics while maintaining professional integrity is a delicate balancing act requiring astute emotional awareness and control. One effective strategy involves cultivating a persona of neutrality and fairness. This means being seen as someone who listens to all sides and makes decisions based on merit rather than personal bias or alliances. This can be achieved by actively listening during discussions, providing balanced feedback, and being transparent about your decision-making processes. Another key strategy is to focus on your emotional responses. Feeling frustrated or defensive when navigating political situations is natural, but recognizing and managing these emotions can prevent you from reacting impulsively and damaging your reputation or relationships.

Building alliances within the workplace is another area where EQ can be particularly effective. Rather than forming alliances based solely on mutual benefit, focus on connecting with colleagues through shared values and emotional understanding. This might involve identifying colleagues who share your commitment to transparency, quality, or innovation and fostering these relationships through regular interactions and support. By aligning yourself with individuals who positively influence the workplace culture, you can create a network that supports not only your personal growth but also the overall health of the organization. These alliances, built on mutual respect and understanding, tend to be more sustainable and less likely to be perceived as self-serving, which can often be a criticism in politically charged environments.

Maintaining personal integrity is perhaps the most crucial element when dealing with office politics. This involves committing to your principles even when it may be easier or more advantageous in the short term to compromise them. Applying EQ in this context means being aware of and true to your profession's emotional values and ethical standards. It also involves having the courage to speak up when necessary, whether to credit an overlooked colleague or to question a decision that conflicts with the organization's values. By consistently applying these principles, you protect your professional integrity and set a standard of behavior that can influence the broader workplace culture.

Navigating office politics with EQ is not about avoiding conflict or competition but about engaging in these dynamics thoughtfully and ethically. It requires a deep understanding of your own emotions and those of others, enabling you to make smart decisions that align with your values and the greater good of your team and organization. As we close this chapter, reflect on how emotional intelligence can transform your view of office politics from a dreaded fact of office life into an opportunity for building more robust, more ethical relationships within your workplace. This perspective is not only beneficial for your career but also contributes to a more positive and productive organizational environment. The next chapter will explore emotional intelligence in dealing with difficult emotions, an essential skill for maintaining professional composure and fostering a healthy workplace.

CHAPTER 9
DEALING WITH DIFFICULT EMOTIONS

Navigating difficult emotions can often seem like trying to find a path through an overgrown forest—daunting, unpredictable, and fraught with the unknown. Among these challenging emotions, anger is particularly complex and known for its intense and sometimes destructive energy. However, when approached with emotional intelligence, managing anger becomes less about suppression and more about constructively understanding and channeling this powerful emotion.

THE EQ APPROACH TO MANAGING ANGER

Understanding the Triggers

Anger, often perceived as just a surge of raw emotion, is more nuanced than that. It is frequently a response to perceived threats or injustices, whether to our self-esteem, boundaries, or expectations. Identifying what triggers your anger is crucial to managing it effectively. This process requires keen self-awareness—a core component of EQ. You can see patterns by reflecting on instances that provoke anger. Perhaps it's a voice that reminds you of past disrespect or a situation where you feel out of control. Recognizing these triggers doesn't remove them, but it does arm you with the knowledge to anticipate and prepare for emotional responses, making them easier to manage.

Cognitive Reappraisal Techniques

Once triggers are identified, cognitive reappraisal is a powerful EQ tool for altering emotional responses. This technique involves changing your interpretation of a trigger situation to decrease its emotional impact. For instance, if a colleague's abrupt email style frequently ignites your anger, reappraising the situation to consider that they might be overwhelmed with work and not intentionally brusque can shift your emotional response from anger to empathy. This reframing dampens the anger and can enhance your relationship with your colleague by fostering a more compassionate viewpoint.

Anger as a Communicator

It's essential to recognize that anger is not just an emotion to be quelled—it's also a communicator. It signals that something important to you may be in jeopardy. Perhaps it signals that your boundaries are being crossed, or it might highlight an unmet need. By listening to what your anger is trying to communicate, you can address these deeper issues more directly. For example, if you find yourself angry every time family gatherings are discussed, it may signal a need for personal space or a boundary about your time. Addressing these needs directly can not only alleviate the anger but also improve your personal well-being and relationships.

Constructive Anger Expression

Expressing anger constructively is an art form that balances honesty with consideration. It involves expressing your feelings and needs without blame or contempt, as the latter often escalate conflicts rather than resolving them. Techniques such as "I" statements allow you to communicate your feelings clearly and openly without triggering defensiveness in others. For example, saying, "I feel frustrated when meetings start late because it affects my schedule," clearly states the problem and your feelings without blaming anyone, opening the door for cooperative problem-solving.

Navigating through anger with emotional intelligence transforms this daunting emotion into a manageable and even helpful part of your emotional repertoire. By understanding triggers, reappraising situations, listening to the deeper messages of anger, and expressing it constructively, you can turn potential conflicts into opportunities for personal growth and relationship enhancement. This approach enriches your emotional landscape and empowers you to handle life's challenges with a greater sense of calm and control.

OVERCOMING ANXIETY WITH EMOTIONAL INTELLIGENCE

Anxiety, a pervasive companion for many, manifests itself in a myriad of ways, ranging from subtle psychological nuisances to profound physical symptoms. It can creep up during a stressful event or linger as a constant shadow over daily activities, often without a clear trigger. Recognizing the symptoms of anxiety is the first step toward managing it with emotional intelligence. Physically, anxiety might present itself as an increased heart rate, excessive sweating, or an unsettling tremor in the hands. Psychologically, it may surface through persistent worry, racing thoughts, or an overwhelming sense of dread. Self-awareness, a core component of emotional intelligence, is crucial in identifying these symptoms. By tuning into your body's cues and observing your thought patterns, you can begin to discern the onset of anxiety. This heightened awareness allows you to address anxiety proactively rather than being caught off-guard.

Mindfulness practices play an instrumental role in mitigating the intensity of anxiety. These techniques anchor you in the present moment, often providing a respite from the relentless worry about future uncertainties or past regrets. Incorporating mindfulness into your daily routine can be as simple as engaging in focused breathing exercises for a few minutes daily. Such practices help recalibrate your emotional state, shifting your focus away from anxiety-inducing thoughts to the calm and stillness of the present. Over time, these moments of mindfulness can extend, allowing you to maintain a more centered and peaceful state throughout the day. Moreover, routine mindfulness can subtly rewire your brain to be less reactive to the stressors that typically trigger anxiety, fostering a more resilient and composed demeanor.

Reframing anxious thoughts is another powerful technique that can transform overwhelming pessimistic predictions into more balanced, rational perspectives. This cognitive strategy involves challenging the automatic beliefs that underpin your anxiety. For example, if you often think, "I can't handle this," try reframing it to "I'm feeling overwhelmed now, but I have managed similar situations before." This reframing helps to break the cycle of negative thinking that fuels anxiety, replacing it with a more empowering narrative. Regular practice of this technique can gradually shift your mindset from one of vulnerability and fear to one of strength and confidence, significantly reducing the psychological grip of anxiety.

Building a supportive network is equally important in managing anxiety. This network should include individuals who understand and empathize with your emotional experiences, offering support without judgment. Sharing your feelings with trusted friends or family can provide emotional relief and valuable perspectives you may overlook when anxious. Additionally, professional help from therapists or counselors trained in emotional intelligence and anxiety management can provide tailored strategies to cope with and reduce your anxiety. These professionals can guide you through various therapeutic techniques, from deep breathing and mindfulness to cognitive-behavioral strategies, helping you build a robust toolkit for managing stress in diverse situations.

Together, these strategies weave a comprehensive approach to managing anxiety through emotional intelligence. By recognizing the symptoms, employing mindfulness, reframing anxious thoughts, and leaning on a supportive network, you equip yourself with the tools necessary to navigate anxiety not just with endurance but effectively and with grace. This proactive engagement with your emotional health paves the way for a more serene and controlled experience, where anxiety does not dictate your life's pace or quality.

THE ROLE OF EQ IN TREATING DEPRESSION

In the intricate dance of emotions and mental health, emotional intelligence offers a unique perspective on managing and treating depression. In this context, one of the most crucial aspects of EQ is emotional awareness, which plays a pivotal role in recognizing the early signs of depression. Often, these signs may be subtle and easily overlooked, such as a gradual withdrawal from social activities, a persistent sense of fatigue, or slight changes in eating and sleeping patterns. By enhancing your emotional awareness, you develop a keener sense of these changes, not only in your emotional states but also in your behaviors and thoughts. This heightened awareness is vital for early intervention, which can significantly affect the course and severity of depression. It allows individuals to seek help at an earlier stage, potentially averting the more profound impacts of long-term depression. Furthermore, understanding your emotional landscape can guide you to more accurately communicate your needs and experiences with healthcare providers, leading to more tailored and effective treatment options.

Self-compassion is another cornerstone of EQ that is particularly effective in combating the harsh, self-critical thoughts that often accompany depression. These thoughts can create a negative feedback loop in which low self-esteem and feelings of worthlessness exacerbate symptoms of depression. Self-compassion involves treating yourself with the same kindness, concern, and support you would offer a good friend. Exercises designed to foster self-compassion include writing yourself a letter of support or speaking to yourself with understanding and care during moments of distress. Practicing self-compassion can help break the cycle of negative self-judgment and replace it with a more gentle and forgiving approach to your struggles. This shift not only alleviates symptoms of depression but also improves overall emotional resilience, making it easier to cope with future challenges.

In therapeutic settings, EQ is increasingly recognized as a valuable tool in treating depression. Therapies that incorporate EQ principles, such as Emotion-Focused Therapy (EFT) and specific techniques in Cognitive-Behavioral Therapy (CBT), can offer practical strategies for patients. EFT, for instance, focuses on helping individuals understand and manage their emotional responses more effectively. It encourages patients to explore and accept their emotional experiences, which can lead to deeper insights into and resolutions of emotional problems, including those contributing to depression. CBT, on the other hand, often includes elements of emotional training that teach patients how to identify and alter negative thought patterns, a skill rooted in emotional intelligence. These therapeutic approaches emphasize the management of emotions in a way that can mitigate depression symptoms and lead to greater emotional health.

Addressing lifestyle factors that impact emotional health is also crucial in managing depression. Regular physical activity, adequate sleep, and balanced nutrition are foundational aspects that profoundly affect mental health. Exercise, for example, not only boosts physical fitness but also directly affects mood, mediated by the release of endorphins, known as "feel-good" hormones. Similarly, sleep affects mood and emotional well-being, and disruptions in sleep patterns are commonly linked with depressive episodes. Nutrition also plays a critical role; deficiencies in specific vitamins and minerals can exacerbate symptoms of depression. By making conscious choices to integrate regular exercise, ensure sufficient sleep, and eat a balanced diet, you are taking proactive steps to support your mental and emotional health. These lifestyle changes, while sometimes challenging to implement, are essential components of a comprehensive approach to treating depression, enhancing the effectiveness of therapeutic techniques and improving overall quality of life.

Incorporating EQ into the treatment and management of depression provides a multi-faceted approach that not only addresses the symptoms but also the underlying emotional dynamics. This holistic perspective fosters a deeper understanding of oneself and enhances the capacity to manage not just depression but also the overall complexities of emotional health.

TURNING ENVY AND JEALOUSY INTO GROWTH OPPORTUNITIES

Envy and jealousy are emotions that most of us encounter at some point in our lives. While often viewed negatively, these feelings can serve as catalysts for personal growth and self-improvement if approached with emotional intelligence. At the root of envy and jealousy are deeper issues such as insecurities, unmet expectations, or perceived disparities in success or happiness. These emotions provide a unique opportunity to examine our innermost desires and the values that guide our lives. By understanding what triggers these feelings, you can address the underlying causes and transform these emotions into productive forces.

For instance, feeling envious of a colleague's promotion may reflect deeper feelings of insecurity about your career progress or dissatisfaction with your current role. Instead of allowing this envy to sour your relationship or impact your self-esteem, use it as a motivator to assess your career path. Are there skills you need to develop or goals you need to set? This introspection can lead to a more focused and motivated career strategy, turning feelings of envy into a springboard for your development.

Shifting your perspective from comparison to inspiration is another powerful way to transform envy and jealousy. When we compare ourselves to others, we often focus on what we lack rather than what we can aspire to achieve. Try viewing others' successes as sources of inspiration rather than benchmarks of inadequacy. For example, rather than feeling inadequate when a friend buys a home, let their achievement inspire you to explore your goals and possibilities in homeownership. What steps did they take that you can learn from? Can their journey offer insights into budgeting, saving, or the home-buying process that you can apply to your life goals?

Developing gratitude is an effective strategy to counter feelings of envy and jealousy. By focusing on abundance rather than scarcity, you can cultivate a sense of contentment with your life's blessings. Gratitude shifts your focus from what is missing to what is present. This can be practiced through simple daily exercises such as keeping a gratitude journal where you jot down things you are thankful for each day or starting your day by acknowledging one thing you are grateful for. This practice diminishes the intensity of envy and jealousy and enhances overall emotional well-being, fostering a more positive outlook on life.

Creating personal growth plans is a proactive way to constructively use the energy from envy and jealousy. Start by setting clear, achievable goals that focus on areas of personal development—career, relationships, health, or hobbies. These plans should be tailored to your aspirations, not shaped by the accomplishments of others. By focusing on your personal growth, you reduce the impact of envy and jealousy, as you are too engaged in your positive journey to dwell on comparisons. These plans also provide a structured path to improvement, making achieving your goals more systematic and rewarding.

By understanding and rechanneling envy and jealousy, you overcome the negativity associated with these emotions and enhance your capacity for emotional resilience and personal fulfillment. This approach alleviates the distress these feelings can cause and fosters a life enriched by genuine self-improvement and contentment.

This chapter has explored the transformative potential of dealing with difficult emotions through emotional intelligence. Understanding the roots of these emotions, applying cognitive techniques to alter our perceptions, and using our feelings as catalysts for personal growth can enhance our emotional well-being and lead to more fulfilling lives. This journey through our emotional landscape continues in the next chapter, where we will delve into the power of emotional intelligence in fostering resilience and thriving through life's challenges.

CHAPTER 10
EMOTIONAL INTELLIGENCE AND SOCIAL MEDIA

In an era where digital footprints are as impactful as physical ones, understanding how to navigate the online world with emotional intelligence is paramount. The internet is a vast expanse of connectivity—a tool that brings knowledge, relationships, and entertainment within easy reach. However, it also presents unique challenges to our emotional health, exposing us to constant information flow and interpersonal dynamics that can be overwhelming. Managing our digital engagement with emotional intelligence ensures that our online experiences enrich rather than deplete our emotional well-being.

PROTECTING YOUR EMOTIONAL HEALTH ONLINE

Digital Detox Strategies

Imagine your mind as a garden. Just as a garden can thrive under the right conditions, so can your mental landscape when given a chance to rest and rejuvenate away from the constant digital buzz. A digital detox, which involves setting aside periods where you deliberately avoid digital devices, can be a refreshing pause for your mind. Initiating periodic digital detoxes can help mitigate the emotional toll of constant connectivity. Start with manageable intervals, like a weekend afternoon without devices, gradually extending to an entire weekend. During these times, engage in activities that nourish your soul and senses—perhaps a walk in the park, reading a book, or a face-to-face catch-up with friends. The key is to create a routine that periodically clears your mental space, allowing you to return to the digital world refreshed and centered.

Curating a Positive Online Environment

The content you consume can significantly influence your emotional state. Just as you are mindful of nourishing your body with healthy food, feeding your mind with content that uplifts and enriches is crucial. Start by evaluating your social media feeds and notice how different types of content make you feel. Unfollow or mute accounts that trigger negative emotions or lead to unproductive comparisons. Instead, intentionally follow pages that inspire and uplift you. Whether it's educational content, motivational speakers, or accounts sharing beautiful images of nature, make your feed a source of positive input. Additionally, consider using features like "screen time" or "content preferences" to actively manage what you see first in your feeds or how long you spend on different platforms.

Recognizing and Managing Online Triggers

Online interactions are laden with triggers that can swiftly stir strong emotions like anger, envy, or sadness. Recognizing these triggers is the first step in managing them effectively. Consider how specific discussions, images, or social media posts make you feel. Are there particular topics or individuals that consistently evoke a strong reaction? Once identified, you can decide how to handle these triggers best. This may mean avoiding certain discussions, limiting exposure to specific content, or engaging in mindful reflection before responding to provocative posts. Developing strategies to cope with these triggers ensures that your online interactions are more deliberate and less reactive, protecting your emotional well-being.

Mindful Consumption of Content

Mindful consumption of online content involves engaging with digital media intentionally and thoughtfully, much like how mindful eating practices encourage awareness and enjoyment of food. Before logging on, set a clear intention for your digital use. Are you looking to relax, find information, or connect with friends? This intention can guide your online activities and make them more purposeful. Additionally, regularly check in with yourself while online. Notice if your actions align with your purpose or if it's time to log off. This practice helps prevent mindless scrolling and ensures your digital interactions are more satisfying and less draining.

Incorporating these strategies into your digital life empowers you to use social media and online platforms in a way that supports rather than undermines your emotional health. By cultivating a balanced and intentional approach to digital engagement, you ensure that your online world is a place of enrichment and positivity, mirroring the emotionally intelligent interactions you strive for in the physical world.

EMPATHY AND KINDNESS IN DIGITAL INTERACTIONS

In the internet's vast, often impersonal space, practicing empathy can sometimes feel like trying to send a comforting gesture through a static-filled screen—challenging yet absolutely necessary. Recognizing the human element behind the digital personas is crucial when we engage online, whether in forums, social media, or email. Practicing empathy online begins with acknowledging that individuals with feelings, struggles, and stories are behind every comment, post, or message. This recognition is the first step toward fostering more meaningful and compassionate interactions. When you respond to others, please take a moment to consider their emotional state. For instance, if someone shares a problem or a challenging experience, instead of offering unsolicited advice or a quick judgment, a simple response expressing understanding or solidarity can go a long way. "I'm sorry you're going through this" or "Thank you for sharing your story" can provide comfort and validation. When engaging in discussions, especially on complex or divisive topics, take a moment to read thoroughly and reflect before responding. If you prefer not to engage, feel free to scroll by, but if you choose to respond, this pause will help you process the words and emotions behind them, fostering a thoughtful and empathetic reply that considers the other person's perspective and feelings.

The veil of anonymity online can often embolden individuals to express themselves in ways they might not in face-to-face interactions. This anonymity can sometimes lead to harsher criticisms or more polarized opinions. However, it also provides a unique opportunity to practice and spread kindness without the bias of preconceived notions based on physical appearance or social status. To maintain kindness and empathy even in heated or challenging discussions, focus on the content of the conversation rather than the person's character. If you find yourself in a tense exchange, remind yourself that there is a real person on the other side of the screen, probably feeling as passionate about the subject as you are. Employing empathetic statements acknowledging the other person's viewpoint can help de-escalate conflicts and lead to more constructive exchanges. For example, statements like, "I see your point, but I think differently. Here's why..." can keep the conversation respectful and focused on understanding rather than winning.

Supporting others online, whether they are friends or strangers, requires a delicate balance of empathy and respect for boundaries. Social media platforms and forums are often places where people seek support and connection, especially those who may feel isolated in their offline lives. When someone reaches out for support or shares a problem, offering a kind and thoughtful response can significantly impact their emotional well-being. However, it's also important to respect personal boundaries and the public nature of online platforms. Keep your responses considerate and supportive, and avoid personal inquiries that may make someone uncomfortable. Suppose someone's situation sounds serious or seems to need more than just online support—in that case, gently encouraging them to seek professional help can be a way of showing care without overstepping boundaries.

Creating positive digital communities is an active and ongoing endeavor that relies on each member's commitment to empathy and kindness. As a member of any online community, you have the power to influence the tone and culture of the space. This can be as simple as posting positive comments, sharing uplifting content, or initiating supportive conversations. You can also participate in or organize online events promoting kindness and understanding, such as virtual meet-ups, webinars on digital empathy, or online support groups. By fostering an environment where empathy and kindness prevail, you help cultivate a digital space that discourages negativity and conflict and promotes a supportive and inclusive community atmosphere. Such communities make the online world more bearable and mirror the kind of real-world interactions we aspire to—respectful, understanding, and enriching.

SETTING BOUNDARIES: THE EQ WAY TO MANAGE SOCIAL MEDIA

In the bustling digital world, where notifications never cease and apps beckon with endless content, setting personal boundaries around social media use is not just beneficial—it's essential for maintaining emotional well-being. Think of these boundaries as the necessary limits you place around a garden to keep it healthy and protected from pests. In the context of social media, these boundaries help safeguard your mental space, allowing for healthier engagement and preventing the all-too-common digital overload. Establishing clear boundaries could involve designated times when you log off completely, perhaps during meals or before bedtime, creating pockets of peace in your daily routine. Another effective boundary is setting specific times for checking social media, which can prevent the habitual, mindless scrolling that often leads to increased stress and distraction. It's also helpful to be selective about what you share and with whom you share it, preserving your privacy and maintaining a sense of personal space. By implementing these boundaries, you protect your emotional health and enhance your ability to engage with digital media in a way that is mindful and fulfilling rather than draining.

Notifications—the constant beeps, buzzes, and pop-ups accompanying modern digital life—demand our attention and fragment our focus, pulling us away from the present moment and into the digital world. Managing these interruptions is crucial for reducing stress and improving concentration. Start by taking inventory of all the notifications you receive across your devices. Evaluate each one for its actual necessity. Does it serve a critical function, or is it merely an interruption? Most devices and apps allow you to customize which notifications you receive, so take advantage of these settings. Consider turning off all but the most essential alerts, such as those for direct messages or appointment reminders. For those you decide to keep, experiment with different alert styles—perhaps a vibration could replace a sound for less intrusion. Another strategy is to use features like Do Not Disturb during hours when you want to ensure focus or relaxation, allowing only priority contacts to reach you. These adjustments can significantly decrease the cognitive load imposed by frequent interruptions, fostering a calmer, more focused mind.

Encouraging a balance between online interactions and in-person connections is becoming increasingly vital as digital platforms become more embedded in our daily lives. While online interactions offer convenience and breadth, face-to-face encounters often need more depth and emotional richness. Each mode of interaction has its unique value—digital communication can keep us connected across distances and provide access to networks that would be otherwise unreachable, but in-person interactions are irreplaceable for their immediacy and richness of emotional and nonverbal cues. To find a balance, make conscious choices about when to text or email and when to arrange a face-to-face meeting. For instance, if a conversation is likely emotionally charged or complex, opting for an in-person discussion can prevent misunderstandings that are too common in text-based communication. However, it's important to recognize that this approach may not be suitable for everyone. Depending on the person's personality, the reverse could be true. Readers need to know themselves well enough to understand what works best for them, whether that's face-to-face interaction, written communication, or another method entirely. Similarly, while it's easy to scroll through social media to catch up on friends' lives, make a point of scheduling regular outings or coffee dates to maintain the depth and vitality of these relationships. This balanced approach enhances the quality of your relationships and enriches your emotional life.

Dealing with harmful or toxic interactions online is, unfortunately, a part of the digital landscape, but handling these situations with emotional intelligence can mitigate their impact. When faced with negativity or hostility, the first step is to protect your emotional well-being. Sometimes, this means disengaging entirely from a conversation or blocking a user. If you choose to respond, take a moment to breathe and compose yourself to prevent a knee-jerk reaction that you might regret. Respond calmly and assertively, sticking to facts rather than emotions, which can help de-escalate potential conflicts. If the interaction occurs within a community or forum, it may also be worth reporting the behavior to moderators, who can take further action to maintain a healthy environment. Remember, you control how you engage with online content and interactions. You can choose to confront, ignore, or redirect negative encounters in ways that preserve your peace of mind and uphold the standards of kindness and respect that are foundational to emotional intelligence.

FROM ONLINE TO IN-PERSON: TRANSLATING EQ ACROSS PLATFORMS

In the digital age, the line between our online personas and real-life identities can often blur, making it essential to maintain a consistent identity across both realms. This consistency is crucial not only for our integrity but also for the authenticity of our interactions. You create a seamless identity that fosters trust and reliability when you align your online presence with your true self, including your core values and beliefs. This alignment ensures that people who meet you in person will encounter the same individual they've interacted with online, eliminating any dissonance or unexpected discrepancies. To achieve this, regularly reflect on your online interactions and posts. Ask yourself if they truly reflect your values and how you wish to be perceived by others. If discrepancies arise, consider adjusting your online behavior to mirror your real-life persona more accurately. This may mean sharing more about your real-life experiences or expressing your genuine opinions more openly, thereby fostering a more authentic online presence.

Translating online connections into meaningful in-person relationships is another nuanced art that requires careful consideration and emotional intelligence. The initial step is to ensure safety and comfort by choosing public meeting spaces and informing a trusted friend about the meet-up details. Once these practical measures are in place, focus on building a genuine connection by bringing the same level of authenticity and interest that characterizes your online interactions. Discuss significant topics during your digital communications to create a sense of continuity and depth. However, be open to discovering new aspects of each other that have yet to be apparent online. This openness can enrich the relationship, providing a fuller understanding of each other and strengthening the bond.

Digital communication skills developed through online interactions, such as clarity and brevity, can significantly enhance in-person conversations. In digital platforms with short attention spans, you learn to convey your messages succinctly and clearly. Apply these skills to face-to-face interactions by being clear about your thoughts and intentions and listening actively. However, remember to appreciate the richer context provided by in-person interaction, which includes tone of voice, pace, and emotional depth, allowing for more nuanced communication. This blend of digital communication skills and the full spectrum of personal interaction creates a dynamic and effective communication style that can adapt to diverse contexts.

The role of nonverbal cues during in-person interactions must be balanced. Unlike online communications, where cues are absent or limited, face-to-face interactions are rich with nonverbal information such as gestures, facial expressions, and body language. These cues often convey more than words can say, providing insights into emotions and attitudes that may not be explicitly expressed. Integrating this aspect into your interactions involves becoming more attuned to these subtle signals. Pay attention to how a person's body language aligns with or contradicts what they say, and use this information to guide your responses. This heightened sensitivity improves your ability to communicate effectively and deepens your empathetic engagement, enriching the interaction and strengthening the relationship.

By bridging the gap between your online and offline worlds through consistent identity, careful translation of digital connections, skillful communication, and sensitivity to nonverbal cues, you enhance your ability to navigate both realms with authenticity and emotional intelligence. These practices enrich your personal interactions and extend the positive impact of your online engagements into your real-world experiences.

As we conclude this exploration of seamlessly integrating online and offline interactions through emotional intelligence, we recognize the impact of maintaining consistency, translating connections, and enhancing communication skills. These strategies ensure that our digital engagements enrich rather than undermine real-world relationships, fostering a holistic approach to social interactions. The next chapter will delve into building resilience through emotional intelligence, a crucial skill for thriving in the face of life's inevitable challenges and changes.

CHAPTER 11
BUILDING RESILIENCE THROUGH EMOTIONAL INTELLIGENCE

In the theater of life, resilience is not merely the ability to bounce back; it is the profound strength that allows us to navigate the storms and still sail forward. It's an emotional agility that transforms obstacles into stepping stones and despair into fortitude.

As we delve deeper into how emotional intelligence underpins resilience, we uncover tools and perspectives that help us endure and thrive in the face of adversity.

THE EQ BLUEPRINT FOR RESILIENCE

Resilience, often visualized as the flexibility of willow trees, which bend in the fiercest winds but do not break, is built on foundational components such as flexibility, optimism, and emotional management. Each plays a vital role in navigating life's inevitable challenges effectively.

Components of Emotional Resilience

Flexibility, the first of these components, involves adapting to changing circumstances swiftly and efficiently. This trait is crucial because it allows you to adjust your strategies and expectations in response to new information or altered conditions, minimizing frustration and setbacks. Optimism, the second component, is the general expectation that good things will happen or that challenges and bad events are temporary setbacks that can be overcome. It is the fuel that keeps hope alive during tough times. Managing emotions, the third component, is the most critical aspect of resilience. It involves identifying, understanding, managing, and healthily expressing emotions. This skill ensures that you remain clear-headed, can make strategic decisions under pressure, and maintain your mental health even during crises.

Developing a Resilient Mindset

Cultivating a resilient mindset requires a paradigm shift to view challenges as opportunities for growth rather than insurmountable obstacles. This perspective is not about denying the difficulty of situations but about embracing them as catalysts for personal development and learning. To foster this mindset, begin by altering your internal dialogue. Shift from a fixed mindset, which assumes that capabilities are innate and unchangeable, to a growth mindset, which thrives on challenge and sees failure as a springboard for growth. This shift is facilitated by self-talk that encourages learning and perseverance, such as "What can I learn from this situation?" or "How can I grow from this experience?"

EQ Tools for Resilience

Several emotional intelligence tools can be instrumental in building resilience. Emotional regulation, for instance, helps you manage and respond to an emotional experience with various strategies that prevent you from becoming overwhelmed. This may involve techniques such as cognitive reappraisal to change the emotional response to a situation or problem-focused coping to directly address the source of stress. Empathy, another crucial EQ tool, involves understanding and sharing another person's feelings, which can enhance your relationships and provide social support during difficult times. Practicing empathy can lead to more meaningful connections and a support network that can offer help and encouragement when you face personal challenges.

Learning from Resilient Role Models

Role models who exemplify resilience can provide inspiration and practical strategies for handling life's challenges. These can be individuals from your personal life, such as a family member or mentor, or public figures whose life stories reflect significant adversity and triumph. Learning from their experiences can offer valuable insights into resilience-building behaviors and attitudes. For instance, studying how a community leader navigated a crisis or how a historical figure overcame personal tragedy can reveal patterns and strategies that you can adapt to your own life. Reflecting on these stories encourages a deeper understanding of resilience and its components, enriching your approach to building your resilience.

We construct a robust tapestry of resilience by weaving these threads together—flexibility, optimism, emotional management, a determined mindset, practical EQ tools, and lessons from role models. This fabric holds firm against the winds of adversity and becomes richer and textured with each challenge. As we explore the multifaceted nature of emotional intelligence, its profound impact on our ability to persevere and flourish in the face of trials becomes increasingly apparent. Let's carry forward this understanding, applying these insights and tools to cultivate a resilience that endures and empowers.

LEARNING FROM FAILURE: AN EQ PERSPECTIVE

Failure, often cloaked in negativity and disappointment, can be one of your most powerful tools for personal growth if approached with the right mindset. The key lies in reframing how you perceive and react to failure. Traditionally seen as a setback or a mark of inadequacy, failure, when viewed with emotional intelligence, transforms into a stepping stone toward success. Reframing failure begins with changing your internal narrative from one of defeat to one of opportunity. For instance, if a project at work doesn't go as planned, consider it a trial run for a more successful future attempt instead of labeling it a failure. This shift in perspective opens the door to learning and growth, preventing the discouragement and self-doubt that often follow perceived failures. It encourages a mindset that values experience as a profound teacher and embraces the lessons that come with each challenge.

Processing the emotions associated with failure is essential in turning setbacks into progress. It's natural to feel disappointment, frustration, or even anger when things don't go as anticipated. However, suppressing or ignoring these feelings can hinder your emotional health and resilience. Allow yourself to experience these emotions fully, but limit how long you let them dominate your state of mind. Techniques such as setting a "worry time"—a period during the day to focus on and process these feelings—can help manage and contain negative emotions. After acknowledging these feelings, it's crucial to move forward consciously. Action steps can include:

- Analyzing what went wrong
- Identifying factors you can control
- Planning how to address these elements in the future

This active approach mitigates the sting of failure and empowers you to take constructive steps toward future success.

Setting realistic expectations is another critical aspect of managing the impact of failure. While ambition drives us to push boundaries and set high goals, unrealistic expectations can set us up for disappointment. Start by assessing your goals to ensure they are achievable and aligned with your current resources and constraints. This assessment involves considering the time, skills, and support available to you and may prompt you to adjust your objectives to fit your circumstances better. Realistic expectations help maintain motivation and commitment, making you less likely to feel overwhelmed or discouraged. Furthermore, they allow for smaller, incremental successes that build confidence and competence, making larger goals more attainable.

Viewing failure as feedback is one of the most constructive ways to deal with setbacks. Every failed attempt is rich with insights about processes, personal limits, and unforeseen variables. By analyzing what these failures reveal, you can make informed adjustments that enhance your strategies and approaches. For instance, if feedback from a failed marketing campaign shows that the target demographic prefers a different communication style, this insight becomes valuable information for crafting future campaigns. Similarly, personal failures, such as not achieving a fitness goal, provide feedback on your methods, discipline, time management, and perhaps even your physical and emotional limits. By embracing failure as a necessary informant, you equip yourself with the knowledge to refine your efforts and enhance your likelihood of future success.

Incorporating these strategies into your approach to failure will shift your experiences from roadblocks to valuable milestones on your path to achievement. This perspective fosters resilience and encourages a lifelong habit of learning and growth—a true mark of emotional intelligence. As you continue to apply these insights, watch as your relationship with failure evolves, transforming your professional landscape and your personal growth trajectory.

THE ROLE OF SUPPORT SYSTEMS IN EMOTIONAL RESILIENCE

In navigating the undulating terrain of life, the support systems we cultivate around us are not only sources of safety but also pillars that uphold our resilience. The intricate tapestry of relationships we weave—whether through personal connections, professional networks, or community ties—plays a crucial role in our ability to face and overcome adversity. Understanding how to build and maintain these supportive relationships is not just beneficial; it is integral to the fortification of our emotional resilience.

Building supportive relationships begins with the deliberate act of fostering reciprocal and nurturing connections. This process involves more than just surrounding yourself with people—it means cultivating relationships rooted in mutual respect, empathy, and understanding. Start by assessing your current relationships. Identify those that provide emotional nourishment and actively contribute to your well-being. These relationships often encourage open communication and emotional honesty, where vulnerabilities can be shared without fear of judgment. Invest time and emotional energy to strengthen these connections by being present during interactions, actively listening, and showing genuine interest in others' experiences. It's also vital to be that supportive figure for others, reinforcing these relationships' reciprocal nature. The goal here is to create a network of relationships that serve as a source of comfort and encouragement, thereby enhancing your resilience.

The importance of seeking professional support must be addressed, especially when the complexities of our emotional landscape exceed the help that non-professional peers can offer. Therapy or counseling can provide a safe space to explore and understand emotions, behaviors, and thoughts with the guidance of a trained professional. These settings offer expertise and an objective perspective that is sometimes necessary for personal growth and emotional management. If you're facing persistent feelings of overwhelm, anxiety, or depression, or if you're struggling to cope with life's challenges, consider reaching out to a mental health professional. This step, often perceived as daunting, is a profound act of self-care that significantly bolsters emotional resilience. Remember that seeking help is not a sign of weakness but a proactive approach to maintaining your mental health.

Community and connection play pivotal roles in resilience by providing a sense of belonging and shared strength. Engaging with a community—based on location, interest, or circumstance—can offer crucial support and validation during tough times. Look for communities that align with your values or interests, such as local clubs, support groups, or online forums. Active participation in these groups can lead to stronger emotional ties and a collective resource of coping strategies and encouragement. Furthermore, communities often provide a platform for sharing experiences and learning from others, which can significantly diminish feelings of isolation and helplessness. If such a community isn't readily available, consider taking the initiative to create one. This may involve starting a support group for a specific cause or organizing community gatherings focused on mutual support and resilience-building.

Finally, the power of supporting others is a remarkable component of building your resilience. Helping others strengthens your relationships and reinforces your sense of purpose and self-worth. Acts of support can range from offering a listening ear to more tangible assistance, such as helping someone needing resources or guidance. Engaging in supportive actions can lead to positive emotional experiences and a heightened sense of community and belonging. It's a reciprocal dynamic; as you support others, you contribute to their well-being and enhance your emotional resilience, creating a virtuous cycle of mutual aid and emotional strength.

As we navigate these strategies, it becomes clear that the support systems we nurture are indispensable to our ability to withstand and adapt to life's challenges. Building and maintaining supportive relationships, seeking professional help when necessary, engaging with the community, and offering support to others are all practices that fortify our emotional resilience. These connections and activities weave a safety net that catches us when we fall and lifts us in times of need, ensuring that we have the resilience to rise and move forward no matter the hardship.

CULTIVATING HOPE AND OPTIMISM WITH EQ

At the heart of resilience lies a robust hope and optimism, essential for navigating life's unpredictable challenges. In this context, hope is not just wishful thinking but a dynamic cognitive process that fuels our journey through difficulties. It involves the expectation that good things will happen and the belief that our actions can positively impact our outcomes. Cultivating a hopeful outlook begins with setting goals that are meaningful and attainable. This process, grounded in emotional intelligence, involves recognizing your strengths and limitations and setting your sights on goals that challenge yet are within your reach. It also includes developing multiple strategies to achieve these goals, which increases the likelihood of success and fosters a sense of agency.

One effective way to nurture hope is to practice what psychologists call "mental contrasting." This involves visualizing the desired outcome and then reflecting on the obstacles that stand in the way. Such a practice enhances motivation and primes you for practical problem-solving. To supplement this, maintaining a "hope journal" can be beneficial. In this journal, record daily entries of your aspirations, the challenges you anticipate, and the strategies you plan to employ. This serves as a motivational reminder of your goals and helps you track your progress and refine your approach, reinforcing a hopeful outlook in the face of setbacks.

The balance between optimism and realism is akin to walking a tightrope. Too much optimism without grounding can lead to disappointment, while excessive realism may curb enthusiasm, hindering motivation and potential opportunities. Emotional intelligence plays a pivotal role in maintaining this balance. It involves being aware of and regulating your emotions to foster a positive yet realistic attitude. An optimist with emotional intelligence embraces positive thinking while being attuned to reality, preparing for various outcomes. To cultivate such a mindset, practice assessing situations with a balanced perspective. Acknowledge the positives without disregarding the potential challenges. This balanced approach preserves your mental energy and prepares you for various possible outcomes, enhancing adaptability.

Gratitude practices are another cornerstone in building optimism and enhancing emotional well-being. By regularly acknowledging and appreciating what you have, you shift your focus from what's lacking to what's abundant. This shift is necessary as it fosters a sense of satisfaction and well-being, which buffers against despair during tough times. Begin by incorporating simple gratitude exercises into your daily routine, such as writing down three things you are grateful for every morning or expressing thanks to someone each day. Over time, these practices can significantly elevate your mood and outlook, broadening your attention to the positive aspects of your life and diminishing the impact of negatives.

Visualizing positive outcomes is an empowering tool that harnesses the power of the mind to foster hope and resilience. This technique involves vividly imagining achieving a goal or successfully navigating a challenging situation. Visualization activates the same neural networks as actual task performance does, effectively priming your brain for success and boosting your confidence. To practice this, set aside a few minutes daily to close your eyes and vividly imagine achieving your goals. Focus on the details—the emotions you feel, the sounds you hear, and the reactions of others. This mental rehearsal enhances your motivation and improves your psychological preparedness for the real-life challenges that await you.

Cultivating hope and optimism through these emotionally intelligent strategies enhances resilience and improves overall quality of life. These practices equip you with the tools to face life's uncertainties with a proactive and positive mindset, ensuring you remain robust and adaptable no matter the circumstances.

As we conclude this exploration into the power of hope and optimism, remember that these qualities are not innate dispositions but skills that can be honed. Through intentional practice and emotional intelligence, you can transform hope and optimism into vital components of your everyday life, enhancing your ability to cope with adversity and your overall emotional and psychological well-being. Moving forward, let these insights guide you as you nurture a resilient and hopeful spirit, prepared to face whatever challenges life throws your way.

In the next chapter, we will explore the realms of emotional intelligence further, uncovering more strategies and insights to enrich and empower your journey through life.

CHAPTER 12
A LIFELONG JOURNEY OF EMOTIONAL INTELLIGENCE

Imagine standing at the edge of a vast landscape, the horizon stretching out to offer a path of growth, discovery, and mastery. This is the terrain of your emotional intelligence, where each step forward enriches your personal and professional relationships and deepens your connection with yourself. As you stand ready to navigate this expansive territory, you must have a map and a compass—tools that will guide you through the intricacies of emotional development. This chapter serves as your guide, helping you to chart the course and mark the milestones of your ongoing journey in emotional intelligence.

SETTING UP YOUR EQ DEVELOPMENT PLAN

Personalized EQ Goals

The first step in any journey is knowing your destination. In the context of EQ development, this means setting personalized goals that not only reflect your current emotional capabilities but are also aspirational enough to stretch your abilities and foster growth. To begin, take a moment to reflect on your recent interactions, both at home and in your professional environment. Where did you feel challenged? What emotional reactions would you like to manage better? You may want to handle workplace conflicts with more calmness, or you may want to offer more profound empathy within your relationships. Using these reflections, set goals that are specific, measurable, achievable, relevant, and time-bound (SMART). For instance, if improving empathy is your goal, you could plan to engage in at least one meaningful conversation per day in which you focus solely on understanding the other person's perspective without rushing to judgment.

Regular Self-Assessment

You must periodically check your map and compass to navigate any journey effectively. In EQ development, this translates to regular self-assessment. This ongoing process helps you track your progress toward your EQ goals and provides critical insights into your emotional growth. Tools such as reflective journaling, feedback forms from peers or mentors, and self-assessment questionnaires can be invaluable. For example, maintaining a daily journal where you record and reflect on your emotional responses can help you see patterns and progress that may otherwise go unnoticed. Over time, these entries will show how far you have come and highlight areas that still need attention.

Incorporating Feedback

No journey is a solitary endeavor, and on your path to enhanced emotional intelligence, the feedback from those around you is as vital as a guide in uncharted territory. Constructive feedback from friends, family, and colleagues provides external perspectives on your emotional behaviors that you might miss. It is essential to approach this feedback with openness and a willingness to learn rather than defensiveness. Consider regular feedback sessions with trusted individuals who understand your EQ goals. Discuss your progress and ask for specific instances where they felt you handled an emotional situation well or areas where you could improve. This feedback can then be integrated into your development plan, adjusting your strategies and focus as necessary.

Long-Term Commitment

Lastly, it's important to view your EQ development as a long-term commitment. Like any profound journey, mastering emotional intelligence is not linear. There will be challenges and setbacks, but each is an opportunity for growth. Embrace the idea that EQ development is a continuous process woven into the fabric of your daily life. It's not a destination to reach but a lifelong journey of learning and adaptation. Integrating EQ practices into your daily routine becomes second nature, part of your ongoing approach to living a fulfilled and emotionally intelligent life.

In navigating these strategies, remember that the emotional intelligence journey is one of the most rewarding treks you will undertake. It promises a transformation of your interpersonal interactions and a profound evolution of your inner landscape. As you continue to explore and apply the principles of emotional intelligence, each step forward enriches your understanding of yourself and others, paving the way for a life filled with deeper connections and more meaningful experiences.

MINDFULNESS PRACTICES FOR CONTINUOUS EQ GROWTH

In cultivating emotional intelligence, mindfulness serves as a vital tool, subtly weaving the fabric of awareness through the tapestry of daily life. Integrating mindfulness exercises into your routine enhances your emotional intelligence and fortifies your mental resilience, allowing for a deeper connection with both the self and others. Let's explore how simple, daily practices can become powerful catalysts for emotional growth.

Mindfulness, in its essence, is the practice of being fully present in the moment, with a gentle and non-judgmental focus on one's thoughts and feelings. To incorporate this into your daily life, consider starting with a simple breathing exercise each morning. As you wake, spend a few minutes in bed focusing solely on your breath—notice the air entering and leaving your body, the rise and fall of your chest, and any sensations that arise. This practice sets a calm, centered tone for the day, tuning you into a mindful state that enhances your emotional awareness from the moment you rise. Take short "mindful breaks" during work or activities as the day progresses. This could be a minute of deep breathing, a focused observation of your surroundings, or a mindful appreciation of a meal. These brief intervals help reset your emotional compass and maintain clarity of mind amid daily stresses.

The intersection of mindfulness and emotional awareness is profound. Mindfulness enriches your understanding of your emotional landscape by slowing down the mental chatter and allowing you to observe your feelings without immediate reaction. This pause is crucial—it provides the space to recognize the emotions themselves, their triggers, and your typical responses to them. Over time, this practice deepens your self-knowledge, equipping you with the insights to manage your emotions more effectively. For instance, if you feel repeatedly anxious in certain situations, mindfulness allows you to notice this pattern and explore its roots in a focused, non-reactive way. Such insights are invaluable, as they form the foundation for building strategies to navigate these feelings more constructively.

Meditation is an essential aspect of developing EQ for many people. Meditation, a practice often associated with mindfulness, involves dedicated periods of concentration to deepen the understanding of the mind and foster a heightened state of awareness and calm. Various forms of meditation are suited to different goals and preferences, making it a versatile tool in your EQ development arsenal. If you need more than meditation, start with some beginner yoga. You get many of the same benefits from yoga, along with the health benefits yoga provides. Focused attention meditation can be particularly beneficial for enhancing emotional intelligence. This practice involves focusing on a single object, breath, or thought, which trains your mind to maintain attention and resist distractions. This ability directly enhances your emotional regulation skills by allowing you to shift your focus away from emotionally disruptive impulses. Another valuable practice is loving-kindness meditation, which fosters compassion and empathy by focusing on sending feelings of love and well-being to oneself and others. This form of meditation expands your capacity to understand and empathize with others, a cornerstone of emotional intelligence.

Encouraging the integration of mindfulness into everyday activities ensures that this practice is not just reserved for moments of quiet reflection but is woven throughout your daily experiences. For example, engage in mindful listening during conversations. This involves fully concentrating on the other person's words, tone, and body language without planning your response while they speak. Not only does this enhance the quality of your interactions, but it also deepens your relational connections by making others feel genuinely heard and valued. Similarly, practicing mindfulness while performing routine tasks—such as washing dishes or walking to work—can transform these moments into opportunities for growth, turning the mundane into gateways of mindfulness that continually nurture your emotional intelligence. These practices ensure that mindfulness is not an isolated exercise but a vibrant, living part of your everyday life, constantly contributing to your emotional growth and resilience.

THE ROLE OF MENTORSHIP IN EQ DEVELOPMENT

Your navigation of the nuances of emotional intelligence can often benefit greatly from the guidance of a mentor, someone who has traversed similar emotional landscapes and can offer insights and strategies based on real-life experiences. Identifying the right mentor, therefore, is a pivotal step in your EQ development. A suitable mentor should possess a high level of emotional intelligence and exhibit qualities such as empathy, patience, and a genuine interest in helping others grow. When seeking out a mentor, look for individuals who demonstrate effective emotional management in challenging situations and whom others look up to for guidance and support. This could be a leader in your workplace, a coach, or a therapist whose approach aligns with your personal growth goals. Engaging with a mentor involves more than occasional meetings; it requires a willingness to be open and vulnerable, sharing your struggles and successes. A mentor can provide tailored feedback, help you see blind spots in your emotional behaviors, and challenge you to push beyond your comfort zones in safe and supportive ways.

Beyond one-on-one mentorship, consider the rich learning opportunities available to leaders in emotional intelligence. Many researchers, authors, and practitioners have shared their insights through books, workshops, and online platforms. Engaging with their work can give you a broader perspective on emotional intelligence, introducing you to diverse theories and applications that may resonate with your personal or professional life. For instance, attending workshops or listening to talks from renowned EQ experts can expose you to new ideas and methodologies that enhance your understanding and application of emotional intelligence. Furthermore, many leaders in emotional intelligence also offer training programs or certification courses that can provide structured learning and professional development opportunities in this field.

Peer mentoring is another enriching avenue for EQ development, one that fosters mutual growth and accountability. This mentoring relationship is typically less formal and can occur naturally within your existing social or professional circles. You and your peer mentor can set goals together, hold each other accountable, and provide mutual support. The reciprocal nature of this relationship allows both participants to practice their emotional intelligence skills, such as empathy, feedback delivery, and active listening, in a real-world context. Organizing regular check-ins with your peer mentor can help maintain momentum and ensure continuous progress. Additionally, peer mentoring creates a safe space for discussing challenges and successes, which can be particularly beneficial for reinforcing learning and encouraging persistence.

Lastly, stepping into the role of a mentor can significantly enhance your emotional intelligence. Teaching is often the best test of understanding, and by mentoring others, you are challenged to articulate and demonstrate the EQ concepts you have learned. The responsibility of guiding someone through emotional development can deepen your self-awareness and empathy. Moreover, as a mentor, you are likely to encounter a range of emotions and situations your mentees present, which can provide fresh challenges and learning opportunities. Mentoring can reinforce your commitment to practicing emotional intelligence, keeping the principles and techniques at the forefront as you advise and support others. In fostering a culture of emotional intelligence through mentoring, you contribute to a community where emotional skills are valued and nurtured, enhancing individual and collective growth.

In these ways, mentorship in various forms plays a significant role in developing emotional intelligence. Whether through engaging with experienced mentors, learning from leaders in the field, participating in peer mentoring, or providing mentorship to others, these relationships enrich your understanding and application of EQ. They ensure that your growth in emotional intelligence is not an isolated endeavor but a dynamic, interactive process enriched by shared experiences and collaborative learning.

CELEBRATING YOUR EMOTIONAL INTELLIGENCE MILESTONES

In personal development, recognizing and celebrating each step of growth in emotional intelligence is akin to pausing during a hike to enjoy the view—it rejuvenates your spirit and prepares you for the next stretch. The act of celebration, often overlooked in our quest for self-improvement, is vital. It not only reinforces positive behaviors but also boosts your morale and motivation. Acknowledging your growth, no matter how small the feat—such as successfully navigating a problematic conversation calmly or finally understanding a colleague's perspective—is essential. These moments of achievement provide concrete proof of your evolving EQ skills. To effectively recognize your growth, make it a practice to reflect at the end of each day or week. Consider maintaining an EQ growth journal where you jot down instances of emotional intelligence you displayed. Regularly reviewing this journal can offer a profound sense of accomplishment and a clear view of your progress.

Reflecting on your development in emotional intelligence is not merely about acknowledging growth but understanding the depth and breadth of your evolution. This reflection involves looking back at where you started, the obstacles you faced, and how you overcame them. Reflection is a powerful tool that provides insights into your personal growth and deepens your learning. For instance, revisiting a past situation where you felt overwhelmed but which you now handle with ease can be incredibly enlightening and encouraging. To facilitate this, engage in reflective practices such as meditation or guided imagery, focusing on your emotional growth. Visualize your past self, recognize your challenges, and compare them with your current state. This practice highlights your growth and instills a sense of gratitude and pride in your accomplishments.

Sharing your story of emotional intelligence development holds untapped power—it can inspire and uplift others struggling with their emotional growth. By openly discussing your challenges, the strategies you used, and the benefits you've experienced, you provide a roadmap for others. This sharing can take many forms, from casual conversations with friends to more structured settings like workshops or social media posts. When you share your experiences, ensure that your narrative is relatable and authentic, focusing on the emotional aspect of your journey. This authenticity makes your story more engaging and impactful, creating a ripple effect of motivation and encouragement within your community. Consider starting a blog or a podcast if you are comfortable with a broader audience. These platforms allow you to reach more people and connect with a community of like-minded individuals, fostering a supportive network.

Setting new milestones is crucial as it ensures that your growth in emotional intelligence is continuous. Once you achieve a goal, setting another, slightly more challenging one is important. This ongoing goal-setting keeps your development dynamic and prevents stagnation. For instance, if you have become adept at managing your emotions during team meetings, the next milestone could involve taking on a leadership role in a high-pressure project. When setting these new goals, use the insights gained from your past achievements and challenges to shape these future objectives. Ensure that these goals align with your overarching life goals, whether related to career advancement, improving personal relationships, or simply becoming more self-aware and content.

As we wrap up this discussion on celebrating milestones and setting new goals in your emotional intelligence development, remember that each step forward enriches your personal and professional life and contributes to a deeper, more meaningful existence. The skills you acquire and refine through this process will serve you in myriad ways, enhancing your interactions and understanding of yourself and others. By continuously engaging with and applying the principles of emotional intelligence, you ensure a lifetime of learning and growth, ready to face whatever new challenges or opportunities life may present.

As we venture into the final explorations of emotional intelligence, remember the importance of integrating these practices into all aspects of your life. This integration solidifies your learning and ensures that emotional intelligence becomes a natural and consistent part of your daily interactions and decision-making processes. Let's continue to build on the foundation we've established, aiming for a future where emotional intelligence informs and enhances every aspect of our lives.

PLEASE TAKE A MOMENT TO SHARE YOUR EXPERIENCE

Now that you have everything you need to take control of your life, it's time to pass on your newfound knowledge and show other readers where they can find the same help.

Your journey through *Emotional Intelligence Unlocked* has given you the tools to understand and manage your emotions better. You've learned to recognize triggers, respond constructively, and improve your relationships. Now, you have the power to help others discover these life-changing strategies, too.

By leaving a review, you can:

- Help someone struggling to find direction in their life
- Support a person seeking to improve their emotional intelligence
- Encourage another reader to embark on their own journey of self-discovery

Your review doesn't just reflect your thoughts—it becomes a beacon for others who are searching for guidance. It can inspire, motivate, and provide the reassurance that they are not alone in their quest for personal growth.

So, if this book has made a difference in your life, please take a moment to share your experience. Your words could be the spark that someone else needs to start their transformation.

Simply scan the QR code below to leave your review:

Thank you for being part of this journey. Your insights and feedback mean the world to me and to countless others who will follow in your footsteps.

Your biggest fan,

Liam Grant

CONCLUSION

As we draw the curtains on this transformative journey through the landscape of emotional intelligence, it's important to reflect on the path we've traveled together. From the foundational concepts introduced in the early chapters to the practical applications discussed for personal relationships, professional environments, and digital interactions, this book has aimed to equip you with the tools and insights necessary to enhance your emotional intelligence.

We've explored the five core components of EQ—self-awareness, self-regulation, motivation, empathy, and social skills. Each plays a vital role in understanding and managing one's emotions and connecting with others. These skills are not just beneficial but essential for fostering healthier relationships, achieving career success, and navigating the complexities of modern communication.

The universality of emotional intelligence is so important. Whether you're looking to improve your relationships, enhance your professional capabilities, or become more adept at managing your online interactions, the principles of EQ are profoundly applicable. They offer a framework for occasional use and a continual guide in every facet of life.

However, enhancing your emotional intelligence is not a destination but a journey that requires persistence, practice, and patience. Please keep engaging with the strategies and exercises provided throughout this book. Regular practice will deepen your understanding and enhance your ability to apply EQ in varied situations.

One of the most significant benefits of developing your emotional intelligence is the resilience it builds. This resilience empowers you to handle life's challenges with greater ease, managing difficult emotions like anger, anxiety, and depression more effectively. It prepares you to face adversities with a balanced perspective and emotional clarity.

I urge you to make a personal commitment to continue this journey of emotional growth. Set personalized goals, engage in regular self-assessment, and, if possible, seek out communities or mentors to support your development. Your emotional intelligence journey is uniquely yours, but it does not have to be solitary.

Moreover, I invite you to advocate for EQ in your own circles and share the knowledge and insights you've gained with others. By fostering a culture that values emotional intelligence, you contribute to a more empathetic, understanding, and resilient society.

As we conclude, I express my deepest gratitude for your willingness to embark on this journey of self-discovery and improvement with me. Your commitment to enhancing your EQ is a personal achievement and a step toward more fulfilling, successful, and resilient lives for us all.

May you continue to embrace the challenges and opportunities with optimism, an open heart, and the powerful tools of emotional intelligence. Here's to a future where we all thrive through the strength of our emotions and the depth of our connections. Thank you, and may your journey be as rewarding as it is enlightening.

BIBLIOGRAPHY

"Emotional Intelligence in Relationships | True You Journal," October 20, 2023. https://www.truity.com/blog/page/emotional-intelligence-relationships.

"Mindfulness and Emotional Well-Being: Strategies to Try," February 25, 2022. https://www.medicalnewstoday.com/articles/mindfulness-for-mental-wellbeing.

BA, Madhuleena Roy Chowdhury. "What Is Emotional Resilience? (+6 Proven Ways to Build It)." PositivePsychology.com, January 22, 2019. https://positivepsychology.com/emotional-resilience/.

Bojic, A. (n.d.). "How to Improve Communication across Generations at Work." Pumble. https://pumble.com/blog/improve-communication-across-generations-at-work/

Chen, Y., Gong, Z. & Wang, Y. (n.d.). "The Influence of Emotional Intelligence on Job Burnout and Well-Being." National Center for Biotechnology Information. https://www.ncbi.nlm.nih.gov/pmc/articles/PMC6916327/

Corbett, Holly. "How High EQ Helps Build An Inclusive Workplace Culture." Forbes. https://www.forbes.com/sites/hollycorbett/2023/02/28/the-emotionally-intelligent-leader-how-high-iq-helps-build-an-inclusive-culture/.

Davis, T. (2020, November). "9 Science-Based Emotion Regulation Skills." Psychology Today. https://www.psychologytoday.com/us/blog/click-here-for-happiness/202011/9-science-based-emotion-regulation-skills

EI Experience. (n.d.). "The Balancing Act of Work-Life Balance." EI Experience. https://eiexperience.com/blog/the-balancing-act-of-work-life-balance/

Forbes Coaches Council. (2019, June 11). "How to Develop Emotional Intelligence Using Mindfulness." Forbes. https://www.forbes.com/sites/forbescoachescouncil/2019/06/11/how-to-develop-emotional-intelligence-using-mindfulness/

Forbes Coaches Council. (2020, April 22). "Understanding the Neuroscience Behind Emotional Intelligence." Forbes. https://www.forbes.com/sites/forbescoachescouncil/2020/04/22/understanding-the-neuroscience-behind-emotional-intelligence/

Forbes Human Resources Council. (2020, September 30). "Why Emotional Intelligence Is Vital for Remote Workers." Forbes. https://www.forbes.com/sites/forbeshumanresourcescouncil/2020/09/30/why-emotional-intelligence-is-vital-for-remote-workers/

Forbes Human Resources Council. (2023, July 18). "The Importance of Emotional

Intelligence at Work." Forbes. https://www.forbes.com/sites/forbeshumanresourcescouncil/2023/07/18/the-importance-of-emotional-intelligence-at-work/

Freedman, J. (2024, February 29). "Dr. Daniel Goleman Explains the History of Emotional Intelligence." Six Seconds .https://www.6seconds.org/2024/02/29/goleman-emotional-intelligence/

Freedman, Joshua. "Case Study: Emotional Intelligence for People-First Leadership at FedEx Express." Six Seconds, January 15, 2014. https://www.6seconds.org/2014/01/14/case-study-emotional-intelligence-people-first-leadership-fedex-express/.

Gottman Institute. (n.d.). "How to Strengthen Your Child's Emotional Intelligence." Gottman Institute. https://www.gottman.com/blog/strengthen-childs-emotional-intelligence/

Grases, Gloria, Maria Antonia Colom, Pilar Sanchis, and Felix Grases. "Relationship of Depression with Empathy, Emotional Intelligence, and Symptoms of a Weakened Immune System." Frontiers in Psychology 14 (October 27, 2023): 1250636. https://doi.org/10.3389/fpsyg.2023.1250636

Grover, R. (n.d.). "The 5 Components of Emotional Intelligence in Today's Workplace." Staffbase. https://staffbase.com/blog/how-to-implement-5-components-of-emotional-intelligence-in-the-digital-workplace/

Hardee, J. (n.d.). "An Overview of Empathy." National Center for Biotechnology Information. https://www.ncbi.nlm.nih.gov/pmc/articles/PMC5571783/

Healthline. (n.d.). "How To Identify And Manage Your Emotional Triggers." Healthline. https://www.healthline.com/health/mental-health/emotional-triggers

Hofmann, S. & Gomez, A. (n.d.). "Mindfulness-Based Interventions for Anxiety and Depression." National Center for Biotechnology Information. https://www.ncbi.nlm.nih.gov/pmc/articles/PMC5679245/

Intelligent Change. (n.d.). "Emotional Intelligence and Its Role in Relationships." Intelligent Change. https://www.intelligentchange.com/blogs/read/emotional-intelligence-and-its-role-in-relationships

Jerus, R. (n.d.). "Emotional Intelligence in Conflict Resolution." Assessments 24x7. https://www.assessments24x7.com/blog/emotional-intelligence-in-conflict/

Kernbach, S. & Schutte, N. (n.d.). "The Impact of Service Provider Emotional Intelligence on Customer Satisfaction." ResearchGate. https://www.researchgate.net/publication/235309364_The_Impact_of_Service_Provider_Emotional_Intelligence_on_Customer_Satisfaction

MA, Courtney E. Ackerman.

MBA, Catherine Moore, Psychologist. "19+ Innovative Ways to Teach Emotional Intelligence to Kids." PositivePsychology.com, February 8, 2019. https://positivepsychology.com/emotional-intelligence-for-kids/.

Patry, P. (n.d.). "Emotional Intelligence and Workplace Conflict Resolution." Global

Mindful Solutions. https://globalmindfulsolutions.com/emotional-intelligence-and-workplace-conflict-resolution/

Riopel, R. (n.d.). "17 Self-Awareness Activities and Exercises (+ Test)." Positive Psychology. https://positivepsychology.com/self-awareness-exercises-activities-test/

Segal, J. (n.d.). "How to Be Emotionally Intelligent in Love Relationships." Help-Guide. https://www.helpguide.org/articles/mental-health/emotional-intelligence-love-relationships.htm

Smith, Sylvia. "Top 10 Effective Communication Techniques for Couples." Psych-Alive (blog), November 13, 2017. https://www.psychalive.org/top-10-effective-communication-techniques-couples/.

Truity. (n.d.). "Emotional Intelligence in Relationships." True You Journal. https://www.truity.com/blog/page/emotional-intelligence-relationships

Urch Druskat, V. & Wolff, S. (2001, March). "Building the Emotional Intelligence of Groups." Harvard Business Review. https://hbr.org/2001/03/building-the-emotional-intelligence-of-groups

Verje, D. (n.d.). "The Impact of Emotional Intelligence on Leadership Success." LinkedIn. https://www.linkedin.com/pulse/impact-emotional-intelligence-leadership-success-deep-verje

Printed in Great Britain
by Amazon